Discovering Mark

THE GUIDEPOSTS HOME BIBLE STUDY PROGRAM

Floyd W. Thatcher *General Editor*
Robin White Goode *Associate Editor*
Bob E. Patterson *Technical Consultant*

EDITORIAL ADVISORY BOARD

Lloyd J. Ogilvie
Senior Minister, First Presbyterian Church
of Hollywood

David A. Hubbard
President, Fuller Theological Seminary

Charles L. Allen
Senior Minister Emeritus, First United
Methodist Church of Houston

Ruth Stafford Peale
President, Foundation for Christian Living;
Vice President, American Bible Society

Myron S. Augsburger
Pastor, Washington Community
Fellowship Church

David L. McKenna
President, Asbury Theological Seminary

Russell H. Dilday, Jr.
President, Southwestern Baptist
Theological Seminary

THE GOSPEL ACCORDING TO MARK

Discovering Mark Tom Mullen
What This Scripture Means to Me Patricia Chapman
The Twelve Disciples Elizabeth Rockwood
Photographs Bruce C. Cresson
Maps Janice Gibson
Book Design Elizabeth Woll
Cover Artist Ben Wolhberg

DISCOVERING MARK

The Guideposts
Home Bible Study Program

GUIDEPOSTS

Carmel   New York 10512

Lyrics from the hymns, *Father of Jesus Christ, My Lord*, by Charles Wesley, and, *Once to Every Man and Nation*, by James Russell Lowell, are used in this volume.

THE GUIDEPOSTS HOME BIBLE STUDY PROGRAM
The Gospel According to Mark:
    1. DISCOVERING MARK
    2. My Working Bible
    3. Knowing More About Mark

All Scripture verses referenced herein are from the King James Version of the Bible.

Designed by Elizabeth Woll.

Printed in the United States of America. Second Printing.

Contents

Publisher's Introduction   7

Preface   9

LESSON 1   13
    What This Scripture Means to Me   29

LESSON 2   31
    What This Scripture Means to Me   43

LESSON 3   45
    What This Scripture Means to Me   59

LESSON 4   61
    What This Scripture Means to Me   74

LESSON 5   76
    What This Scripture Means to Me   89

LESSON 6   91
    What This Scripture Means to Me   104

LESSON 7   106
    What This Scripture Means to Me   120

LESSON 8   122
    What This Scripture Means to Me   134

The Twelve Disciples of Jesus   136
The Miracles of Jesus in Mark   153
The Parables of Jesus in Mark   153
The Harmony of the Gospels   154
Palestine in the Time of Jesus   157
The Travels of Jesus in Mark   158
Judean and Galilean areas in the Time of Jesus   160

Publisher's Introduction

As a writer, John Mark would feel very much at home in the literary genre of today. His economical use of words, direct style, and storytelling ability are appealing to modern readers.

The words seem to tumble from Mark's pen as if he could hardly wait to get the story down. His use of "straightway" and "immediately" almost thirty times indicate his extreme sense of urgency. And yet his meticulous attention to details, especially those expressing the feelings and attitudes of Jesus, give us insights at times that are not available in the other three Gospels.

While the Gospel of Mark has its own particular identity, it is of great importance to us, as students of God's Word, because it is generally considered to be the first Gospel to be written and the first eyewitness account of the actions and words of Jesus. We are not able to pinpoint the actual time of writing, but many leading authorities believe it was sometime after A.D. 50 and before the fall of Jerusalem in A.D. 70, possibly around A.D. 65–67.

And in putting together this first eyewitness account of the drama of Jesus' words and actions, Mark had a peculiar advantage. As the son of Mary, a prominent early Christian who lived in Jerusalem, he had the opportunity of intimate fellowship with many of Jesus' followers. Then he is mentioned briefly as being with Paul and Barnabas, his cousin, on their first missionary journey. But it was on that trip that Mark incurred Paul's displeasure by leaving them early and returning home.

Mark's name surfaces again as Paul and Barnabas plan their second missionary journey. Barnabas wanted to take Mark along, but Paul was adamant in not agreeing to it, so they split up—Paul going one way with Silas while Barnabas and Mark went another way. We get word later on, though, that the rift between Paul and Mark was apparently healed. In Colossians 4 Paul writes that Mark "sister's son to Barnabas" was with him, and, later, Paul tells Timothy that "Only Luke is with me. Take Mark and bring him with thee: for he is profitable to me for the ministry" (2 Tim. 4:11).

In writing his eyewitness account Mark also had the advantage of an intimate relationship with the Apostle Peter. The earliest Christians believed that Peter shared his vivid recollections of all Jesus said and did with Mark who then recorded them carefully in his Gospel. Certainly, we get a clue as to the close relationship between the two men when Peter refers to him as "my son" (2 Pet. 5:13).

It seems likely that Mark wrote his Gospel in Rome, and it conveyed a positive message of hope to Christians there and across the world who daily faced imprisonment and death because of their faith in Christ. He wanted them to be able to walk in the footsteps of Jesus throughout the three and one-half years of His ministry, to be present at His death and resurrection, and then experience the presence of the risen Lord as their companion in trial and suffering.

At the same time, Mark makes it clear for those of us who wrestle with our hopes and fears in the drama of life over 1,900 years later that the Jesus he introduced in the opening words of his Gospel as "the Son of God," is the Jesus of Calvary about whom the Roman soldier said, "Truly this man was the Son of God," and is the same Jesus about whom the "young man" at the sepulchre said "He is risen; he is not here."

In the lessons we come to now you will see that this gifted Gospel writer is always pointing us in the direction of Jesus from whom we today receive power to live and witness for Him in all sorts of circumstances. Our confidence can always be secure in the assurance that He gives power to all who receive Him (John 1:12). And later, Paul reassures us and validates our status when he writes, "For as many as are led by the Spirit of God, they are the sons of God" (Rom. 8:14).

Preface

Thomas à Kempis, in his classic work, *The Imitation of Christ*, advises his readers to concentrate upon Christ as He is revealed in the Gospels. "Let our foremost resolve," he says in Book I, Chapter I, "be to meditate upon the life of Christ."

We hope these lessons encourage the same goal. Mark is the story of Jesus: "The beginning of the gospel of Jesus Christ, the Son of God" (1:1). However, in a careful examination of this earliest Gospel, we see Jesus in a different light than Matthew, Luke, and John perceived Him. While all the writers give us similar details about Jesus' life, Mark includes some information that only someone very familiar with Him could have known. The emotions of Jesus, His spontaneous reactions, even His inner responses are reported. Mark enables us to see Jesus, as Olympic broadcasters might put it, "Up close and personal."

Examining the life of Jesus is an important enterprise. Most Christians know individual stories about Jesus, or they are familiar with a few scattered texts. Far fewer, however, have undertaken what this study encourages, namely, to look carefully at the words, deeds, and personality of Jesus. It is my hope that this study will allow us to confront Jesus in a *fresh* way.

Robert Louis Stevenson maintained that if we use our imagination and read the Gospel "freshly like a book, not droningly and dully," we will be startled and moved. To the degree that these lessons enable us to read Mark "freshly," they will have been successful. When we look at Jesus "up close and personal" in Mark, we can receive certain general impressions.

Jesus was a *popular* teacher and healer. Mark shows that Jesus acquired a large following quickly, and crowds besieged Him wherever He went. The crowd is also the background against which Jesus makes quick decisions and dramatic actions. While healings were sometimes done in private, Jesus had a reputation that attracted large numbers of people.

At the same time it was the presence of the crowd that was a threat to the Pharisees, and on at least two occasions Mark indicates that Jesus' life would have been endangered earlier if the Jewish authorities hadn't feared the reaction of the crowds. Indeed, it was Jesus' popularity that caught the attention of the Pharisees and Sadducees in the first place. Had Jesus taught and healed in private in a way that didn't threaten the religious establishment, they wouldn't have paid much attention to Him at all.

For Jesus, however, the crowds were to be ministered to, and not to be a source of power and authority. He saw them as "sheep without a shepherd," and they came to Him for help. But Jesus knew He could not depend upon the masses of people for support and authority.

For this reason, He chose a few, the twelve disciples, to nurture and train for the extension of His ministry. Jesus continually called them apart for reflection and instruction, but finding time and space for "disciple-building" was not easy. Readers of Mark can easily sense the frantic pace and keen sense of urgency that surrounded Jesus and the twelve disciples. In 6:31, a verse that only Mark records, we read that "many were coming and going, and they had no leisure."

So Mark's Gospel captures a mood of crowd pressure and rapid movement. We know how the story ends, but we still can feel that an explosion is waiting to happen from the very beginning of the book.

Looking at Jesus "up close and personal" enables us to share the frustrations and disappointments He felt about the twelve disciples. Again and again, they simply didn't understand what Jesus meant by either His words or deeds. From the safety of the twentieth century, we may feel the urge to shake them, as if they were naughty children, for being so obtuse and self-centered. But had we been there I wonder if we would have reacted differently.

We may experience one dimension of the miracle Jesus wrought in building a church on this small band of weak, self-absorbed not-too-bright followers. In the Gospel of Mark we see the disciples "up close and personal." Their portraits are unretouched—we see them warts and all.

Jesus' humanity is revealed in Mark as He confronts the Pharisees and labors with His disciples. Mark leaves no doubt that his Gospel is about a divine figure, the Son of God. However, his story describes Jesus' moments of frustration, occasions of anger, and times of sorrow. Mark shows us a Jesus who is fully man as well as fully God.

In a class at Earlham College which I have taught for twenty years, we often perform an exercise with Mark that reveals Jesus as fully man and fully God. I ask my students to make a list of modifiers they feel describes the Jesus who appears in a series of selected paragraphs from Mark's Gospel.

When Jesus was relating to children, they saw Him as "tender" or "loving." As He out-smarted the Pharisees, a student might describe Him as "shrewd" or "clever." They saw Jesus as "angry" or "frustrated," possibly even "petulant," after reading the passage about the cursing of the fig tree. Jesus in the Garden of Gethsemane was described as "lonely," "afraid," or "courageous."

This composite picture of Jesus allows His humanity and His divinity to come into focus for the students. Now the class could better understand why those closest to Jesus had so much difficulty seeing His fullness.

When we read Mark, we also come to realize that we are seeing Jesus "through a glass darkly." We see Him through other eyes, not just our own. We also begin to understand that no matter how faithful we try to be as careful readers, we can never fully *know* Jesus except as an act of faith. We can call him "Lord," and we can follow Him, but Jesus— the God-man—cannot be fully comprehended.

It is my hope that in studying Mark, you will feel and experience the Presence of Jesus in a new way. That is why any useful study must necessarily be accompanied by prayer. Jesus, "up close and personal," cannot be found by the limitations of words on paper. But when Jesus comes *into our experience*, we can know for certain that He will walk with us across our own Galilees of daily life.

LESSON 1
MARK 1:1—2:12

The Jesus Explosion

Open up my mind, Lord, that I might receive and understand this lesson. AMEN.

In the winter of A.D. 64–65, a great fire broke out in Rome. It burned for six days and nights, destroying huge sections of the city. Emperor Nero, who is remembered for fiddling while Rome burned, was rumored to have been responsible for the fire. But Nero blamed the Christians, who were generally unpopular anyway and had frequently been accused of promoting seditious ideas. A reign of terror followed, and Peter and Paul were probably among its victims. Christians were crucified, torn apart by wild beasts in the arena, and burned at the stake. It was a time of unbelievable suffering.

Shortly after this terrible ordeal, Mark's Gospel appeared. It's not hard to see why. Christians were facing persecution and martyrdom, and many were asking a crucial question: Why risk dying for their faith? It was a time when the remembered facts about Jesus needed to be written down. It was a matter of life and death.

Over and over again we hear of a "secret" that must be kept until the right time comes. Mark knew the "secret." His readers within the Christian community knew it too, but the Gospel of Mark was written to show why that which is obvious to insiders (that Jesus is the Christ) is a mystery to others.

If we read the Gospel the way the earliest Christians

The Gospel background.

13

did, it would be like watching a re-run of a tense true-to-life drama. Even though we would know the outcome, remembering the events and recalling the danger would rekindle our excitement and faith.

Preparing the way.

Mark's opening words show that the Christians of his day knew exactly who Jesus was: "The beginning of the gospel of Jesus Christ, the Son of God" (1:1). Jesus was not simply a good man who died a martyr's death. He was and is God among us, and His words and deeds continually amazed those around Him—particularly those who did not know His full identity.

"We know who Jesus is," Mark seems to be saying, "but the Pharisees, the Sadducees, the common folk, at times even the disciples, did not. That's why Jesus was rejected and killed. But *we* know, and therefore we will follow Him, even to death."

So, Jesus moves through Mark's Gospel almost incognito. He is always more than He appears. But although the other actors in the drama are only half aware of the Person with whom they are dealing, Mark has already taken his readers into confidence in his opening statement.

John the Baptist.

Mark's readers also recognize the connection he makes between who they know Jesus to be and Old Testament predictions of the Messiah. Jesus did not come into a vacuum. Mark shared the view with other Christians that Jesus is the climax of history, and in Mark's Gospel, John the Baptist appears on the scene like an Old Testament prophet announcing the arrival of the long-awaited Messiah. Most certainly John is the fulfillment of the four-hundred-year-old prophecy, "Behold I send my messenger, and he shall prepare the way before me"...(Mal. 3:1). Mark's readers would readily identify John with Elijah by the way he dressed and by what he ate (1:6). He came out of the wilderness to prepare the way of the Lord (1:7).

The times were ripe for a Messiah. Palestine was under Roman military and civil occupation. The common people were oppressed and neglected. Political agitators preached violent rebellion, and most of them were promptly executed. The Pharisees, who were supposed to provide religious leadership, were instead preoccupied with pious posturing and rule-following at the cost of authentic spiritual living and ministry.

A location frequented by religious pilgrims for baptism in the waters of the Jordan River.
While the Jordan is the stream where John was baptizing, we cannot be certain of the actual location where Jesus was baptized. However, it is thought the site was probably at a ford a short distance north of where the river flows into the Dead Sea.

Mark tells us that John had a substantial following: "...there went out unto him all the land of Judea, and they of Jerusalem" (1:5). Vast crowds of people went to hear John. He was the leader of a genuine religious revival. Yet, his words shocked his listeners, "There cometh one mightier than I after me, the lachet of whose shoes I am not worthy to stoop down and unloose" (1:7). To remove sandals was the work of a slave! Mark's readers, however, understood. As great as John was, they knew he had been the preface to the Living Word, Jesus Christ.

The message of John the Baptist was part of the preparation. He preached confession, repentance, and baptism, for the time when to receive Jesus as the Christ would require three responses: a recognition of separation from God (confession), a radical turn toward God (repentance), and a fresh spiritual dedication (baptism).

Mark's readers understood this point. They knew that one reason many people failed to recognize Jesus as the Messiah was because they weren't prepared. The same is

15

[Above] *A view of the traditional Mount of Temptation as seen from Ancient Jericho. The site is in the barren Wilderness of Judea where Jesus fasted forty days and was tempted by Satan. This desolate and rocky area begins just a short distance east of Bethlehem and Jerusalem and slopes steadily down to the Dead Sea—a body of water fifty-three miles long and almost ten miles wide. It lies 1,286 feet below sea level.*

[Right] *The Wilderness of Judea, the general area of the activity of John the Baptist and near Qumran. It was at Qumran, approximately eight miles south of Jericho, where the first of the Dead Sea Scrolls were discovered in 1947.*

true today: many of us cannot receive Christ as Lord because we too have leap-frogged over the three vital steps of spiritual preparation.

Thoughtful readers of Mark often ask why Jesus needed to be baptized, particularly since John's baptism was one of repentance. After all, Jesus had not sinned. Why should He be baptized? Mark saw the baptism of Jesus as the moment when His call was defined. Jesus is an adult throughout the Gospel of Mark. It was assumed that He had grown up in Nazareth and faithfully discharged His duties to family and community. But Jesus' baptism signaled the beginning of His ministry, as the voice from heaven announced, "Thou art my beloved Son in whom I am well pleased" (1:11). There's an echo here of the words of the Psalmist hundreds of years before, "Thou art my Son; this day have I begotten thee" (Ps. 2:7).

John the Baptist represented a movement back to God, and Jesus identified Himself with that revival. At His baptism Jesus accepted the calling God had given Him. The words of James Russell Lowell's hymn capture the drama of the occasion:

> "Once to every man and nation comes the moment to decide in the strife of Truth with falsehood, for the good or evil side."

It was a dramatic moment: "the heavens opened" and the "Spirit descended upon him like a dove" (1:10). But in Mark's Gospel little time is spent basking in the glory of these moments. He reports that the Spirit drove Jesus out into the wilderness where for forty days He was tempted of Satan (1:13). Unlike Matthew and Luke, Mark does not give us any additional details of Jesus' temptation except to say that He was with "wild beasts; and the angels ministered unto him."

Jesus' mountaintop baptism experience, followed immediately by His struggle with Satan in the wilderness, models a pattern that many of us have encountered in our own lives. We've heard the voice of God, and responded with commitment and service. But our "highs" have often been closely followed by "lows." We have gone to places or met people who resisted our efforts, tried our patience, or tempted us with unlimited opportunities to compromise our callings. One young minister, for example, described

Calling and testing.

his experience by saying, "My first church was a wilderness because it tempted me to be a nice, friendly, pleasant, and totally irrelevant human being."

One reason Jesus continues to speak to our condition today is that He is intimately acquainted with the temptations we face.

Jesus' ministry is launched.

Mark records the beginning of Jesus' ministry in 1:14. He sets a fast pace in telling the story. In fact, if this drama were made into a movie, it would clearly be an action film. Mark writes with urgency. His Gospel is a series of episodes that are loosely tied together. Some incidents are told with considerable detail. Other events are noted with only a brief summary to show a connection.

"Now after that John was put in prison, Jesus came into Galilee" (1:14). To leap into Jesus' ministry with so little comment about John's arrest startles our thinking. It is like saying, "Otherwise, Mrs. Lincoln, how did you enjoy the play?" We want to exclaim, "What do you mean 'after his arrest'? We didn't even know he was in jail! What happened?"

Mark doesn't bother to tell us. He simply reports the launching of Jesus' ministry in the few words that summarize the Lord's message, "The time is fulfilled, and the kingdom of God is at hand; repent ye, and believe the gospel" (1:15). Note the mood and tense of these words: *Now,* the immediate present, is the time. To "believe" is to give oneself in trust and obedience to God who is making Himself known in the words and deeds of Jesus. The sense of immediate urgency expressed here is characteristic of Mark's terse writing style.

We experience a similar sense of urgency when we rush through a crowded airline terminal. A voice booms over the loud-speaker, "Passengers holding tickets on flight 109 to Boston should check in at gate 18. This is a final boarding call."

Those who hold tickets on flight 109 will run through the airport—if they hear the words. Jesus' summary too, was clear and succinct and generated enormous urgency among those who would listen.

Jesus calls His disciples and us.

The calling of the first four disciples has been a favorite passage for preachers from the day it first appeared in writing. It not only captures the urgency that pervades the

The Sea of Galilee figured prominently in Jesus' ministry. This body of fresh water, surrounded by mountains, is heart-shaped and is approximately twelve miles long and five miles across at its widest point.

Capernaum and Bethsaida on the north shore were key fishing communities in the time of Jesus.

Gospel, but it also provides a model for all Christians (1:16–20).

Here we see Jesus moving purposefully along the shore of the Sea of Galilee, probably at Bethsaida. First He sees Simon and Andrew fishing, and when He said, "Come ye after me, and I will make you become fishers of men," they "straightway forsook their nets and followed him." Jesus then went on a little farther along the shore and saw James and John mending their fishing nets. Mark now tells us that "straightway he called them: and they left their father Zebedee in the ship with the hired servants, and went after him" (1:16–19). The word "straightway," translated "immediately" in later versions, is a favorite with Mark. Used as it is here and throughout the Gospel it expresses the urgency and immediacy of the action taken.

It is hard for twentieth-century people to understand what appears to be the reaction of the four fishermen. We live cautious lives. When young people interview for jobs, their first few questions are often about pension plans and life insurance. By contrast, the response of these disciples seems impulsive, almost irresponsible.

There is not reason to assume, however, that these four men were at this moment seeing Jesus for the first time. There is indication in the Gospels of Matthew and Luke that the four had previous contact with Jesus. And there is every reason to assume that they were ready to respond. Their immediate response does not mean they were being impulsive.

It clearly does convey, however, the radical and bold nature of discipleship. The fact that the first four persons called were fishermen *hooks* us. They had had no training to become disciples and witnesses.

Lack of qualifications can never be an excuse for refusing to follow Jesus. "I'd like to be your disciple, but I have no college degree." Nonsense! "I've always stayed in the background, you see, so if you don't mind..." Even so, follow Jesus. It was Lincoln who said, "God must love common people because He made so many of them." It was Jesus who chose ordinary human beings to be His disciples.

The selection of disciples is also an invitation to companionship with Jesus, a calling into a new kind of community. The Kingdom of God has been announced and now, "straightway," there is work to be done. Discipleship is not a private matter but a shared adventure. While answering God's call is never a thoughtless act, it is more like falling in love than it is like figuring out a math problem.

Why some people, like the four fishermen, respond and others do not remains a mystery. Robert Raines in his book *New Life in the Church* tells how William Larimer Mellon, Jr. read a magazine article about Albert Schweitzer who, at age thirty, had put aside careers in music, writing, and teaching to go to Africa as a medical missionary. After reading the article Mellon felt "called," and without a moment's hesitation he ran to tell his wife that he was going to medical school and when he graduated he would settle down somewhere and become "a good country doctor!"

Were Mark telling the story, he would have written: "And immediately Mellon went to Tulane University and straightway founded a hospital in Haiti." We can't help but wonder how many others read the same article and merely put it aside, or just thanked God for Albert Schweitzer. But to William Larimer Mellon, Jr., it was a personal call from God. Jesus said, "Follow me," and he did.

Ruins of the ancient synagogue at Capernaum. Jesus established the headquarters for His Galilean ministry in this crossroads city located on the north shore of the Sea of Galilee and a short distance west of where the Jordan flows into the sea. Capernaum was a busy fishing and commercial center in Jesus' time.

The ruins of the synagogue visible here date back to the third century A.D. It was built of white limestone. Recent excavations below these ruins have uncovered a synagogue constructed of black basalt—the kind of building materials used in Jesus' time. It is speculated this could have been the building in which Jesus taught.

It was no accident that Mark used a common fishing term in describing Jesus' promise to make them "fishers of men." In the Greek language in which the Gospel was written it means to "take alive," and it describes catching fish in such a way that they would still be alive when brought to shore for sale. The colorful metaphor used here illustrates how the disciples and Jesus were to be companions in the ongoing task of calling others, loving and caring for people, and announcing that God's new day had dawned. Their mission was "to take people alive."

As Mark's story moves swiftly and dramatically toward its climax on the cross, Jesus is presented as a man of action, constantly moving about, challenging opponents,

On the road with Jesus.

21

and entering synagogues to proclaim the Good News. The first stop on this journey was a synagogue in Capernaum where Jesus established a pattern for His ministry that was repeated over and over: combining teaching and healing (1:21–28).

Parenthetically, it is rather interesting to note that a visit today to the ancient site of Capernaum enables the visitor to view the beautiful ruins of an ancient synagogue—a white limestone structure, which dates somewhere between the second and fifth century. However, recent excavations immediately below this building have exposed a black basalt structure, which in all probability is an earlier synagogue. Pottery found at this level dates to the first century A.D. It is very likely this is the synagogue where Jesus taught.

The way Jesus' ministry unfolded makes a lot of sense. First, He was called and tested. Next, He chose disciples. Then, He began His teaching and healing in the most logical place, the synagogue. In those days Jewish synagogues had no permanent teacher. The ruler of the synagogue could ask any competent person to read and expound Scripture. Jesus was an itinerant teacher, and local synagogues provided a convenient pulpit. And in this beginning phase of His ministry, before the religious leaders became hostile toward Him, He was free to enter the synagogues and speak openly. This He did, for as Matthew wrote, "Jesus went about all Galilee, teaching in their synagogues..." (Matt. 4:23).

Mark reports that the people were "astonished" at His teaching. Today we might say that Jesus "blew their minds." Why? Because He taught "as one that had authority, and not as the scribes" (1:22). In contrast, the scribes always began their teaching by quoting as many authorities as possible, usually introducing their lessons with the phrase, "There is a teaching." By contrast, Jesus depended upon His personal authority for credibility.

There is a joke within academic communities that if you quote only one source, you have committed plagiarism. If you quote several sources, you have done research. The scribes sounded as if they were guilty of both plagiarism and research. Their teaching lacked authenticity and failed to be convincing, while Jesus' message had the ring of truth.

Now while Jesus was teaching in the synagogue that day, a mentally deranged man approached Him trembling with fear. The term "unclean spirit" is commonly used in the New Testament for a demon. Demon possession was thought to be responsible for many forms of sickness and misery. Human beings were at the mercy of demons unless they were protected by a stronger spiritual power. When persons were possessed, they often functioned as if they had split personalities. They might speak as if they were the demons themselves, as indeed the poor man in this account did.

The healing of a man with an unclean spirit.

What an odd twist! The first time Jesus is recognized as the Messiah after His ministry began, was by this demon-possessed man, "I know thee who thou art, the Holy One of God" (1:24). But Jesus quickly ordered him to be silent, "Hold thy peace, and come out of him" (1:25). Again, Mark answers here a crucial question, which his whole Gospel addresses: "Why wasn't Jesus recognized as the Son of God during His time on earth?" At this early stage Mark shows that Jesus was known by the forces who had the most reason to fear Him—the demons.

A belief generally held by the people in those days was that the reign of the Messiah would mark the end of demons. Jesus, therefore, was an ultimate threat to demons and their powers to possess people. There were other exorcists around, but the demons themselves would be able to identify the authentic Messiah from the frauds.

The response of the people to Jesus' expelling the demon from this man is significant. Just as the people in the synagogue were *astonished* that Jesus taught with authority, so were they amazed at His ability to heal. From our perspective, with almost 2,000 years of Christian experience behind us, their verbal response seems strange, "What thing is this? What new doctrine is this? For with authority commandeth he even the unclean spirits, and they do obey him" (1:27).

We are tempted to scoff at the skepticism and lack of faith expressed by the people in the synagogue that day. Yet, we are in a position similar to those first-century people. Our problem is like theirs: How can we rise above a second-hand experience of Jesus Christ and become first-person channels of God's power and grace? Even today, authentic, vital, and challenging Christian faith invariably astonishes and amazes people.

Those of us brought up in the church forget how fresh and alive the Gospel message is to new Christians. Barbara Robinson's hilarious and touching book, *The Best Christmas Pageant Ever*, reminds us. Her book captures how a family of ragamuffin children respond to the Christmas story that was totally new to them. They worry about Mary and become angry at Herod. They called the Wise Men a bunch of dirty spies. And in the process of acting out the story, their lives were changed.

Mark shows us that the common people, who didn't fully know who Jesus was, were nonetheless conscious that He was somebody special, "immediately his fame spread abroad." Jesus' reputation as an authoritative teacher-healer sent shock waves "throughout all the region round about Galilee" (1:28).

A private miracle.

Then what did Jesus do? "...forthwith [immediately], when they were coming out of the synagogue, they entered into the house of Simon and Andrew" where He performed a private act of healing (1:29). The incident takes place in Peter's home in Capernaum, apparently situated close by the synagogue. The story as told may have come from Peter's own recollection. It shows how Jesus' healing miracles were not done in order to increase His fame. Sometimes crowds were present; at other times, Jesus healed in the presence of only a few.

In both the private and public healing events, however, there was a common denominator—Jesus healed without elaborate ceremony. In the synagogue before the congregation He gave a simple verbal command, and the demon-possessed man was healed. Later, in the seclusion of a private home, Jesus took Peter's mother-in-law by the hand and lifted her up, and her fever, probably malarial, left her. Ordinary exorcists, then and now, frequently employed complicated incantations and magical rites.

But Jesus' healing miracles were devoid of "show biz." The power was in the Person, and He made the healings fresh and genuine.

Show and tell.

Later that evening Peter's house was surrounded by

people seeking healing, for they recognized Jesus as a doer and not just a talker. Throughout Mark's Gospel he records more of Jesus' deeds than he does Jesus' words. After all, ideas don't have to be told. They can spring up independently. The *idea* that God loves us might occur to any thoughtful and spiritually minded person. But an *act* of love has to be reported in order to make a difference.

It is "actual" love, not "ideal" love, that counts. The words from a song in *My Fair Lady* illustrate the point. In that musical play the heroine expresses her impatience with talk about love and repeatedly exclaims, "Show me!"

The deeds of love Jesus performed were different than what Eliza Doolittle in *My Fair Lady* had in mind, but the principle of showing and telling was the same. No wonder "all the city was gathered together at the door" (1:33). Many of us work hard to "get a crowd out" by promoting a program with gimmicks or advertising a performance. We sell people and market beliefs and products with everything from television commercials to green stamps. By comparison, Jesus' ministry of word and deed was sufficient in itself. There was no need for the hype that accompanies so much of our actions. Jesus never called a press conference.

A time apart.

The next morning, after the energy-draining outpouring of compassion the night before, Jesus felt the need to be alone in prayer "...rising up a great while before day, he went out, and departed into a solitary place, and there prayed" (1:35). Elton Trueblood wrote in his remarkable little book *Confronting Christ*, "The fact that He did not feel self-sufficient was one mark of His divine vocation. Furthermore, the fact that He prayed makes His life more relevant to ours. Prayer is something which He and we have in common."

In Mark's Gospel, we see Jesus frequently praying alone. In times of stress, temptation, and decision, He turns to God for guidance and strength. The minute we categorize Jesus as a "man of action," Mark reminds us that the source of His amazing teaching and healing sprang from His practice of continual prayer.

Simon Peter and his friends, however, soon found Jesus and interrupted His quiet time with the news that "All men seek for thee" (1:37). Jesus responded immediately. A paraphrase of His words may more clearly capture their meaning: "Let's hit the road, to places we haven't been before, for this is my task" (see 1:38). His calling made Him sensitive to human need, whether it was for telling the Good News or demonstrating it. By his actions, Jesus shows us prayer is not a substitute for living the Christian life. Prayer prepares the Christian for service; then empowers the Christian to serve.

On the road again. So Jesus set out, preaching in the "synagogues throughout all Galilee." Mark describes His travels in one verse (1:39), but since Jesus went all over Galilee, it must have taken Him several weeks to complete His journey.

Along the way a leper came and asked for healing. This is the third account of an individual healing in the Gospel. It focuses on the role faith plays in the process more clearly than the first two healings do. The leper acknowledges Jesus' power when he says, "If thou wilt, thou canst make me clean" (1:40). This was a great hope, for no disease was more feared in those times than leprosy. It carried the same psychological fear that a pronouncement of cancer carries today. It also had a terrible social stigma.

Lepers were banished from fellowship with friends and peers. They were forced to live alone, and were ordered to go around with torn clothes and bared heads. Whenever they approached other persons, they had to shout the warning, "Unclean! Unclean!" Lepers experienced double jeopardy—both physical pain and personal humiliation.

But Jesus physically touched this leper, and did not worry about His own health or status. He violated the law and then said, "Be thou clean." Jesus knew that if the leper spread the news of his healing, it would become more difficult to move freely about the country. So He "sternly" charged him to say nothing. But the leper who had been healed went out and told everyone, and people "came to (Jesus) from every quarter" (1:45).

This incident illustrates Jesus' wholistic ministry. He healed the leper's physical illness, but He was equally concerned with the man's need to re-enter society. So Jesus insisted that the leper go through the Mosaic ritual of cleansing so that he would no longer be an outcast (1:44).

The same, by analogy, is true today. Someone may be healed by surgery or counseling, but that person may continue to feel embarrassed by its scars. A woman may recover from a mastectomy and still feel incomplete. A man may overcome a drinking problem and continue to wonder if friends will ever trust him again. Health is more than the absence of disease. It is also a positive attitude, and Jesus knew that a leper is finally cured only when he no longer *feels* unclean.

Mark's fast-moving account of Jesus' ministry brings Him back to His headquarters in Capernaum. By now the scene described is a familiar one: Jesus, the teacher-healer, is in a house and the crowds are literally pushing and shoving to enter. As Mark puts it, "…there was no room to receive them, no, not so much as about the door" (2:2).

What happened next was an incident that most of us brought up in Sunday school know well (2:1–12). In our primary classes we often made little cardboard houses with removable roofs. Then we acted out the story of how four men dismantled the roof in order to lower a paralyzed friend down to Jesus to be healed. It was and is an effective way for children to learn both about the compassion of Jesus and the persistent faith of the paralytic's friends.

Mark wants us to see more than the obvious, however. It is, indeed, a story of healing by Jesus, the fourth individual example recorded in the Gospel. But it is different from any other healing miracle Mark records.

It is the only healing account in the Gospel in which Jesus connects illness and sin. In that day, sickness and sin were closely associated, and the belief that sin caused illness was commonly held. The book of Job and several of the Psalms seem to reflect that view. Even today, people in pain often ask, "What did I do to deserve this?" Here, Jesus addresses that particular mind-set, and He does so to the complete surprise of the scribes who were present.

If this healing miracle had been like the others, Jesus' opening words probably would have simply been, "Be healed." Instead, Jesus said to the paralytic, "Son, thy sins be forgiven thee" (2:5). His words carried a double meaning, for He was speaking to the paralyzed man and delivering a message to the scribes.

Had Jesus simply healed the man, it would have been one more observable act of compassion. But He pronounced forgiveness, and to do so violated acceptable practice and long-standing Hebrew beliefs. He had stopped healing and started meddling! It was an axiom of Jewish faith that only God could forgive sins. For any human to

The healing of the paralyzed man.

The beginning of hostile opposition.

claim to do so was unequivocal blasphemy, for which the law (Lev. 24:16) mandated the penalty of death.

The nit-picking scribes had been waiting for just such a moment. They had caught Jesus in a public statement so outrageous they were sure it would work against Him. But Mark's account suggests that Jesus knew exactly what He was doing. His act of healing was more than a simple compassionate deed—it was a sign of His divinity. His words combined with His deed in a way that confounded the scribes, "…that ye may know that the Son of man hath power on earth to forgive sins, (he sayeth to the sick of the palsy) I say unto thee, arise, and take up thy bed, and go thy way into thine house" (2:11).

Jesus had caught them in their own trap. Any wandering preacher could mouth the words, "Your sins are forgiven," as dangerous as such pronouncements might be. But when the words were linked with an act of healing, it provided proof of Jesus' authority. Since the scribes believed that sickness and sin went together, Jesus in effect said to them, "If sin caused this man's paralysis, then his healing is evidence that My ability to forgive sins is genuine."

In twentieth-century America we treat forgiveness lightly, even the forgiveness of God. We seem to share Voltaire's attitude when he said, "God will forgive me; that's His business." That is a perspective very different from what Jesus demonstrated here. Claiming the authority to forgive sins was no light matter and forgiving them was a costly act. This confrontation was the beginning of the scribes' and Pharisees' outright hostility toward Jesus. It is the first of fifteen controversies between Jesus and orthodox Judaism that Mark gives us in his Gospel. At this time Jesus signed His own death warrant. The religious leaders did not recognize who He was, but One who could speak for God was a clear threat to the wooden legalism they represented. On that point, they were absolutely correct.

Thank You for forgiving not only the sins of the man disabled with palsy, but my own sins as well! AMEN.

WHAT THIS SCRIPTURE MEANS TO ME—Mark 1:1–2:12

One warm spring day we planted a small olive tree in the patio of our Southern California home. It was positioned so we could keep track of its growth through the tall windows that framed the fireplace on the east end of the living room.

The early morning sun streamed in through those windows, but as time passed and the olive tree grew, its branches began to filter out the penetrating rays. At first the shade was sparse, but with each passing year we were sheltered more and more from the sun.

One day I was having my devotions in the living room. It was quiet in the house—the girls were on their way to school and my husband was at the office. Suddenly I felt impressed with the presence of the Lord in the room. I got up off my knees and walked, still in a prayerful mood, to the end of the living room, and looked at the olive tree. I had been telling the Lord that I was open to the fullness of His Spirit and to fill me in any way He chose. I wanted to be open to whatever God had for me.

Without warning, a gust of wind shook the little tree violently for a few moments, and then it was still and quiet again. As I reflected on what happened, it seemed to me that God was present in this incident. I felt that He was speaking to me in a very real and special way as I remembered that the oil of the olive berry was a symbol of the Holy Spirit, as is the wind. God had, I believed, answered my prayer with the assurance that He was indeed with me now in His fullness.

This was an amazing experience for me. Nothing like that had ever happened before to me, nor has it since. I know now that I must have felt like the people in the crowd when Jesus healed the paralyzed man who had been let down through the roof while Jesus was teaching. Mark described their reaction this way, "…they were all amazed, and glorified God, saying, We never saw it on this fashion before."

Jesus was an amazing man. He seems to have rushed headlong into His ministry. Yet, no matter how busy He was, Jesus never seemed hurried. He always had time to stop and help or heal. It seemed that for Him any interruption was an opportunity to minister. So often, though, we react differently and become frustrated over what we think of as interruptions. Our tendency is to feel inconvenienced by an interruption without realizing that it may be an opportunity.

Mark paints a whirlwind picture of Jesus' busy days. He tells us that one day Jesus walked along the shores of Galilee and called Simon, Andrew, James, and John from their fishing boats to become His disciples—fishers of men. The next Sabbath, they went to the synagogue where Jesus cast demons out of a man. Later that same day, Jesus and these four men went to Simon Peter's home, where they found his mother-in-law suffering with a fever, and Jesus healed her. And before the day ended, people brought their sick and diseased, as well as those possessed with demons, for Him to heal. That was all in one day!

The very next morning, they left for a preaching tour. As they went from place to place, they encountered a leper, whom Jesus healed. Then the paralytic man was let down through the roof of the house where Jesus was teaching. He next went to the seaside and taught the multitude there. After that He called Levi to follow Him, and then went to his home that evening for dinner.

No one ever made an appointment with Jesus, and no one was ever turned away. Jesus always had time, even in the midst of the busiest days, to help people—to minister to their physical and spiritual needs. What a man He was! What a model for us in our Christian life and ministry!

Sometimes God speaks in a dramatic way to us as He spoke to me through the olive tree and the whirlwind. Sometimes He touches the suffering and heals. At other times He doesn't seem to speak at all. Yet, His presence is with us. We have His assurance that our prayers are answered and our needs will be met, for He loves us and cares for us. And we can be certain that as we seek Him out, He will minister to each of us in His way and in His time.

LESSON 2
MARK 2:13—3:35

The Eye of the Storm

Open my eyes, Lord, that I might see You in this lesson. AMEN.

Those who stereotype Jesus as meek and mild have not read the Gospel of Mark with their eyes open. Any prudish, soft images of Jesus we might have are shattered as we read chapters two and three. He is far more than a gentle shepherd, holding lambs and touching children. Jesus is the eye of a storm, the center of controversy, a man so dangerous to the Jewish religious leaders that they plot to murder Him.

In Lesson 1 we saw that hostility toward Jesus began to flare when He healed the paralytic in Capernaum (2:1–12). From that point on, the scribes and Pharisees followed Him wherever He went, waiting for some slip of the tongue or outward error as grounds to accuse Him. They were like "truth squads" in political campaigns who trail candidates everywhere, looking for reasons to discredit them. Simply put, the Jewish religious leaders set out to get Him because He advocated a new law, one that put people and their needs ahead of sterile and impersonal rules.

Jesus did not intend to antagonize the scribes and Pharisees. He didn't begin each day by saying to Himself, "What can I do this morning to upset the religious estab-

The "wrong kind" of people.

lishment?" Yet, were the King James Version of the Bible written in today's slang, everything that Jesus said and did seemed to "ticketh them off."

Given His calling to preach, teach, and heal, conflict with the entrenched religious authorities was inevitable. Jesus never went *out* of His way to pick a fight, but as He went *along* His way, controversy erupted.

The opening scene in our lesson has Jesus walking along the shore of the Sea of Galilee at Capernaum in the midst of a great crowd of people. Mark wrote, "...all the multitude resorted unto him." This was why Jesus chose Capernaum in Galilee as the headquarters for His ministry. Located strategically on the highway from Damascus west to the Mediterranean Sea, this busy city was an important center of commerce. Here Jesus could mingle with all kinds of people, and wherever people were He was attracted to them.

But part of the problem centered around the people who were drawn to Jesus. Here we see Him selecting Levi, a tax collector, to be His disciple (2:14). This made no sense at all to the Pharisees, because tax collectors were despised, and not without cause. The common people never knew how much they really owed because the tax collectors squeezed out all they could and kept any amount over and above what the law required. To choose Levi as a disciple was like a mayor selecting the meanest man in town for city council.

That wasn't all. Jesus associated with riffraff, going so far as to eat with them (2:15). To the Pharisees it was unthinkable for Jesus to eat and drink with such bad characters as the "publicans and sinners." Jesus was actually socializing in this scene with persons who were both spiritual and society rejects. And in doing so, Jesus became embroiled in His second controversy with the religious establishment.

As we read these words in Mark, the inclusiveness of Jesus is obvious. Yet our own tendency to divide persons into categories of "good" and "bad" is sometimes as blatant as the Pharisees.

For example, a certain large church became excited about evangelism. It created a master plan that sent teams of church leaders into most parts of the city to distribute literature and make personal contacts. Two sections of the city, however, were not targeted, one mostly black and the other white but very poor. Their "evangelism" was not intended for all, only for some. This stands in stark contrast to Jesus' ministry in that *all* kinds of people, even tax collectors, can follow Him, not just our "own kind."

Next we see the scribes and Pharisees trying one of the oldest tricks of dirty politics: guilt by association. When they accused Him of eating with bad characters, He reminded them that sinners needed His help, "They that are well have no need of the physician, but they that are sick. I came not to call the righteous, but sinners to repentance" (2:17). Apparently, "righteous" persons, like the Pharisees, didn't think there were compelling reasons for spending time with Him. Jesus simply outsmarted them with His reply, and the scribes and Pharisees were left in the awkward position of sounding like the American Medical Association criticizing a doctor for making too many house calls!

Not only did Jesus associate with publicans and sinners, he continually violated certain long-standing religious customs. Fasting is singled out in Mark 2:18–20 as we see Jesus involved in His third controversy. Fasting was, and is, a legitimate spiritual discipline. Many Jews practiced it as preparation for the long-awaited Kingdom of God. John's disciples fasted, the Pharisees were quick to point out, so why didn't Jesus and His followers fast (1:18)?

The "wrong kind" of religion.

Once again the Pharisees demonstrated their spiritual blindness by deliberately trying to cause dissension between the followers of John and those of Jesus. They fasted to parade their piety, but Jesus put fasting in perspective because God's New Order had already begun with His coming; this was a time for celebration, not self-denial. It called for dressing up and feasting as if you were going to a wedding, not for wearing sackcloth and long faces. According to the law, wedding guests were exempt from the regular requirements of fasting.

This incident is a healthy reminder to Christians that joy is an acceptable human emotion, and laughter is characteristic of Kingdom people. Unfortunately, joy is not one of the marks of faith usually attributed to Christ's followers by the secular world. H.L. Mencken once said that "Puritanism is the haunting fear that someone, somewhere is having a good time." Sadly, this kind of "puritanism" is often equated with "Christianity," just as the Pharisees saw fasting as a mark of religious commitment. Jesus, in contrast, invited us to His party, and celebration is as important to a full Christian experience as self-denial. Wouldn't it be grand if we could sometimes think of the church the way one child did. She said, "Church is the place where God goes when He wants to have a good time."

In Chapter 2:20 Jesus hints at His eventual death, "But the days will come, when the bridegroom shall be taken away from them, and then shall they fast in those days." This was a statement Mark's first century readers were sure to understand. But here too, Jesus is separating His message and ministry from Judaism and what it had become. Jesus had not come to patch up an old religion. His message was fresh and sparkling.

He makes this clear in his comparisons about garments and wineskins (1:21–22). New cloth that has never been shrunk will tear away from old cloth when a patched up garment is washed. And new wineskins are pliable and stretch, and can accommodate new wine as it ferments and emits gases that cause pressure. On the other hand, old, stiff wineskins burst under the pressure of fermenting new wine.

Dr. Lloyd Ogilvie brings Jesus' analogy up to date for us when he tells of visiting Beirut, Lebanon several years ago as part of a Holy Land tour. On one occasion the group was meeting with Lebanese Christians and sharing what Christ had done in their lives. The translator struggled to make each witness clear in spite of the colloquialisms used by the Americans.

One woman had a particularly difficult time being understood. She said that before she was liberated by Christ, she had been a grim, inflexible, unbending old bag—someone who let rules and regulations dominate her life. She would shut out anyone who did not measure up to her rigid standards.

The term "old bag" confused the translator, but once he understood, he was able to phrase the idea in Lebanese. Then everyone laughed and nodded in comprehension. It was obvious that there were "old bags"—rigid, unbending folks in Lebanon, even as in America. The fermenting new wine of Jesus Christ cannot be contained in worn-out, stiff, rigid containers.

Just as Jesus spoke to the rigidities of Mark's time, so does Mark's record of His words puncture our "old bags" today. We are to be uncompromising yet flexible Christians who are always open to fresh truths from the Lord.

Jesus now moved out into the countryside, and the Pharisees nailed His disciples for another technical violation: picking corn on the Sabbath. They were hungry, and what would be a harmless act any other day of the week provoked the fourth controversy, because they were accused of breaking the Sabbath (2:23–28).

Corn-picking and nit-picking.

There are some thirty-nine categories of work that are prohibited on the Sabbath and four of these are reaping, threshing, winnowing, and preparing meals. Mark says they began "to pluck the ears of corn" (2:23), but Luke's account of the same incident adds that "they did eat, preparing a meal, rubbing them in their hands" (6:1). In other words, they were technically guilty of reaping, threshing, winnowing, and preparing a meal. We can visualize the Pharisees, popping up from among the corn stalks, pointing their fingers at the disciples, and yelling, "Gotcha!"

But Jesus let the air out of their balloons as quickly as they had blown them up. He reminded them of their own tradition—how David (no less!) had eaten bread when he

Harvesting and gathering wheat—here accomplished as it has been throughout the centuries. There are many references to this kind of activity in the illustrations and parables of Jesus.

was hungry that had been exclusively reserved for priestly consumption (1 Sam. 21:3–6). And, Jesus reminded the scribes that David ate the bread for the most basic of reasons; he and his companions were hungry. "There are," Jesus is saying, "exceptions to the rule!" Furthermore, the *spirit* of the law must be considered. If rules make human life better, they are to be kept. If not, they are to be rejected. We are not to make an *end* out of a *means*: the Sabbath is made for human beings, not human beings for the Sabbath (2:27).

If Jesus had stopped there, He would have won the argument and the grumpy Pharisees would have sulked away licking their wounds to wait for another chance to attack Him. His final words on the subject, however, provided fuel for the fire His enemies were building: "Therefore the Son of Man is Lord also of the Sabbath" (2:28). Jesus had done it again. Just as He had earlier claimed authority to forgive sins, here He assumed the right and power to redefine the Sabbath. It was as if He were saying "Let's not be silly about this day and how it is to be observed. Let's celebrate it in the right way and for the right reasons. Take My word for it."

Our misuse of the Sabbath—for Christians, it would be the misuse of Sunday—is usually a different problem than the one the Pharisees had. We often err in the opposite direction and still miss Jesus' point. Jesus is saying that the day set aside for God is a time for personal renewal and spiritual regeneration. His saying that "the Sabbath was made for man" does not license us to observe it in the frantic, pleasure-obsessed manner in which many of us attack Sunday. We may dutifully attend church, but then fill the day with so many recreational and work activities that our energy is depleted and our spirits drained. It is no longer a day of rest and renewal.

It's okay to buy food on Sunday when we need to do so, but to use Sunday as a primary shopping day is something else. Recreation can be a renewing experience for a family, or it can drain energy and destroy congeniality. Ask any family with small children who take a long drive on a hot day just how spiritually renewing that is! Jesus invites us to reserve the Sabbath for spiritual restoration, not catering to self-denial or self-indulgence.

High noon in the synagogue.

When Jesus refuted the Jewish religious leaders, He

only intensified their opposition. The following Sabbath He did what was customary for Him—He entered again into the synagogue (3:1) even though by then it was risky. Present that day was a man with a withered hand and, coincidentally, a deputation of Pharisees. We don't know whether the man was a trap set for Jesus by the Pharisees or not. But the words in the second verse seem to imply that he was, "And they watched him, whether he would heal him on the Sabbath day; that they might accuse him."

It was a tricky and volatile situation for Jesus. It would have been easy for Him to merely postpone the healing. After all, there was no emergency, and to heal the man in the presence of the Pharisees was to risk a showdown. It was "high noon" in the synagogue.

Jesus made a bold move by asking the man to come out of the crowd and step forward. And as He had done before, Jesus challenged His opponents with the spirit of their own tradition. He asked, in so many words, "Which is more important? To observe empty custom, or to help this poor man?"

The silent response of the Pharisees was like poison gas hanging in the air. The King James Version of the Bible says "they held their peace" (3:4). Jesus stared at them "with anger, being grieved for the hardness of their hearts" (3:5). This must have been quite a stare! He was outraged at their unfeeling stubbornness and stupidity. Their only response to His soul-piercing queries, "Is it lawful to do good on the Sabbath days or to do evil? to save life or to kill?" was silence. Their religion was a lifeless form with no heart.

Jesus asked the man to extend his hand, and in an instant "his hand was restored whole as the other." The moment of truth had arrived. It was a dramatic moment that exposed the moral bankruptcy of the Pharisees and moved Jesus one step closer to Golgotha. Mark tells us (3:6) that the Pharisees went out and made a deal with the Herodians—their despised enemies—as how best to get rid of this itinerant rabbi who dared confront them. In our language we would say they "put out a contract" on Jesus.

As the plotters conspired to kill Jesus, He left the synagogue and went to the shore of the Sea of Galilee. He probably felt the need for a retreat with His disciples so He could renew Himself spiritually. Mark, however, indicates that the retreat was not to be. A great number of people

The work goes on.

followed Him, coming literally from every corner of Palestine—from as far south as Idumaea to the northern cities of Tyre and Sidon in Phoenicia. The pressure of the crowds was so intense that Jesus had a small boat ready in case He needed to escape being crushed (3:9).

Obviously, Jesus had great popular appeal. It is equally obvious that this popularity both impressed and worried the Pharisees. But Jesus Himself did not take it very seriously. Mark's earliest readers who read his Gospel after the crucifixion had happened, knew that the crowds mentioned here did not save Jesus from the cross. Neither their size nor their intensity indicated commitment. Most people were there to get help—for healing, for exorcisms, for words of comfort. But they didn't know who Jesus really was, only that He responded to their needs.

Once again, the ones who recognized the Lordship of Jesus were the "unclean spirits" who "fell down before him, and cried, saying, Thou art the Son of God" (3:11), but He forbade them to tell anyone else. The crowds in Roman-occupied Palestine were waiting for a kingly, nationalistic Messiah who would lead them to freedom and political power. But Jesus' Messiahship was different. He served and loved people who had no clear idea of His divinity.

Mark's Gospel reminds us that Jesus definitely could have instigated a political revolution. His speech was trenchant and compelling, and He verbally overwhelmed His opponents. He was a healer—an imposing and inviting man who attracted huge crowds. We don't fully appreciate the enormity of His temptation to give the people what they wanted because we're studying these events almost two thousand years after they happened. Mark's first-century readers, however, certainly understood better than we do, that for Jesus to withstand temptation and choose His way was a significant moral and spiritual decision.

The redemptive fellowship.

Moving from the seaside to a mountain, Jesus completed His selection of twelve disciples (the group is listed in Chapter 3:16–19). Jesus' choices were puzzling because the men He picked were quite average. He chose four common fishermen (Peter, James, John, and Andrew), a tax-collector-outcast (Levi, also called Matthew), and a fanatical nationalist, a Zealot (Simon the Canaanite). Such persons could scarcely be described as spiritual heavyweights. The rest weren't anything to brag about either.

They were an unlikely and diverse group with not very much in common except their loyalty to Jesus. He risked a lot in bringing together these twelve very ordinary men—each with his own agenda and concept of how a Messiah should behave.

And discipleship had its own agenda. Being a disciple of Jesus would mean more than just hanging on and having one's needs met—it would mean commitment, obedience, and loyalty. And those would be great challenges to meet, because Jesus was getting deeper into trouble every day. He'd already been branded a heretic, a sinner, and a loose-living gadfly. To borrow a metaphor from the stock market, there was no reason to be bullish on Jesus.

Jesus' time away from the crowds was brief, and His return home, probably Capernaum, thrust Him immediately into the same crush of humanity He had left. Mark reports that He had no opportunity even to eat (3:20) because of the pressure of His work. The response of Jesus' friends, reported next, is curious. They said, "He is beside himself" (3:21). They thought Him insane and out of His mind. Why His friends had such an extreme reaction, we do not know for sure. Possibly it was because He didn't take time out of His busy schedule even to eat. Perhaps it was out of concern for His well-being, the way we sometimes insist that a loved one is working too hard. Or Jesus' friends and family may have been worried about His—and their—reputation. After all, what did the neighbors think?

From the mountain to the multitude.

We can understand their reaction when we consider our attitudes toward those whose behavior seems unconventional to us. Take Gandhi, for instance. Time and distance have transformed him into a modern saint, but his behavior and life-style disturbed those closest to him. Honor may come to a missionary who chooses to live in poverty in an African village, but he or she is just as likely to be misunderstood and regarded as not quite "normal."

In the comfort of our late twentieth-century Christian society we frequently criticize the things that don't seem normal to us. We tend to feel that anyone who worships, reads the Bible, or acts differently from us, is out of his or her mind. But Jesus had an inclusive message—a gospel of love and concern—and this was not "normal" to the religious leaders of His day.

A newspaper reporter once did a story on Mother

Teresa and her ministry of healing among the destitute poor in India. He focused on one of the young nuns who worked with Mother Teresa. He followed her throughout an exhausting 14-hour day and wrote his story with a personal, human interest slant. He watched and took notes as she bathed children, treated festering sores, fed babies, and ministered to the dying. At the end of the day, he commented to the weary woman, "I wouldn't do what you do for a million dollars." Her reply was classic, "Neither would I."

Jesus and those who closely follow Him march to the tune of a different Drummer. His will was centered in God's will, and according to the usual standards of behavior, He seemed unbalanced, even to His friends and family.

The "unforgivable" sin.

Following closely after the accusation of His friends that He was not in His right mind, Jesus was confronted with another blow—His fifth controversy involving the source of His power. A delegation of scribes that had traveled all the way from Jerusalem to see what was going on accused Jesus of practicing black magic, "He hath Beelzebub, and by the prince of the devils casteth he out devils" (3:22). They charged Jesus with being demon-possessed and said that His power came from the devil. With impeccable logic Jesus refuted their accusations. He pointed out that Satan would not harm himself, "How can Satan cast out Satan... if Satan rise up against himself, and be divided he cannot stand, but hath an end" (3:23–26).

At this particular encounter, Jesus raised an issue that has troubled many Christians since Mark recorded it. In 3:28–29 Jesus says that "All sins shall be forgiven unto the sons of men, and blasphemies wherewith soever they shall blaspheme: but he that shall blaspheme against the Holy Ghost hath never forgiveness, but is in danger of eternal damnation."

These words trouble us because, on the surface, Jesus sounds out of character. He seems to be saying that God's forgiveness has limits. The Good News is that no one is outside God's Grace, but these words declare there is an unforgivable sin.

A closer look, however, reveals the subtle irony of this statement. Forgiveness depends upon our ability to repent.

Resistance to the Spirit of God, such as the scribes demonstrated, precludes forgiveness. Jesus is not saying God refuses to forgive, but that some people are unable to *accept* forgiveness. They are closed to it simply because they are incapable of seeing their need for forgiveness. The unforgivable sin is the one for which we have no willingness to repent. To experience forgiveness we must be open to it.

The family of Jesus.

Almost as troubling is the final scene of Chapter three. Here Jesus appears to be indifferent toward His own family. They come looking for Him, and when Jesus learns of their presence, He seems to ignore them (3:31–35). Instead of rushing to them for a happy and sentimental reunion, He uses the occasion to make a point. And His point has to do with the nature of true kinship.

Brotherhood and sisterhood, He says, are based on common obedience to God. As close as we may be to our parents and blood relatives, the quality of kinship Jesus calls for is more intimate. To be brothers and sisters in Christ is to go beyond natural biological relationships.

Mark's earliest readers would have easily understood this thinking. Not only were they persecuted by the world, they were frequently rejected by their families. For them, the Christian community was often their primary family. Common obedience to Christ was the single most important bond they shared.

Occasionally, Christians today experience first-hand what Jesus meant. For example, one young couple was riding on an airplane, bouncing around because of air turbulence, and making not-entirely funny jokes about meeting their Maker. This caused them to speculate what would happen if both of them died while their children were small. They had brothers, sisters, and other blood relatives who could adopt their children and provide them with physical and parental support.

However, as they thought through this hypothetical situation, the couple decided not to depend on their "natural" family connections. They wanted their children to be brought up in the church, to be nurtured in their own faith, and to have the daily experience of a Christian home life. Their "natural family," they concluded, was less able to meet these needs than certain families in their congregation who were their "brothers and sisters in Christ." Shortly thereafter, they made appropriate legal arrangements with a family in their church fellowship.

The tie that binds, says Jesus, goes beyond blood relationships. It is a shared commitment to a common Lord.

From Lessons 1 and 2 we see that Mark pulls no punches as he records the story of Jesus. He reminds his readers and us of the head-on collisions Jesus had with the religious establishment, and he writes down many of the tough sayings Jesus uttered.

Jesus ministered to the crowds who came for help, but His hope was invested in the small band of unlikely disciples He had chosen. Jesus' presence brought comfort and compassion to many, and simultaneously provoked controversy and crisis with others. His ministry was like a storm blowing across Palestine, a storm that forever changed the lives of all who either loved or despised Him. And Jesus continues to confront and challenge us today whenever we invite Him along on our walk through life. We may follow Him or not, but once He enters our experience, like the people of Palestine, we can no longer ignore His presence, and we can never be the same again.

Lord, help me to walk in the truths I learned in this lesson, especially, to put people and their needs ahead of rules, ahead of my schedule, ahead of the things I think are so important. AMEN.

WHAT THIS SCRIPTURE MEANS TO ME—Mark 2:13–3:35

"Anyone seen my Sunday School quarterly?"

"Where is my blouse?"

"My shoes aren't shined!"

"Are Lou and Harry coming for dinner again?"

"Help me with the table. I want to get it set before church."

"Hurry up. We'll be late for church again."

"I don't wanna go. I can't find anything to wear."

"Come on, you guys. Get in the car!"

And in this kind of frantic atmosphere the "happy family" rushes off to church. Is this all too familiar scenario a part of Sunday morning in many Christian homes? I suspect it is, and perhaps it is so common that we've come to think that that is the way it should be. But I wonder—is there anything that could be done to change this? Should we even try? The answer, I believe, is a resounding YES!

If we were visiting Israel today, we would probably hear a cab driver or a vendor or even a soldier say something about it being "three days to Shabbat," or "two days to Shabbat."

What do they mean by this countdown? What is Shabbat? A simple inquiry would tell us that they are counting the days until their Sabbath. That would probably seem strange to us because I doubt that many Christian families would be counting the days until Sunday—the Lord's Day. There might be some, but I've never heard anyone do it.

There is a great deal in Scripture about the Sabbath that emphasizes the specialness of the Lord's Day. In this passage in Mark, the legalists—the Pharisees—are very upset because according to their rules, Jesus' disciples broke the Sabbath by picking corn for food, "Why do they on the sabbath day that which is not lawful?"

But we read in our Scripture lesson that Jesus defended the actions of His disciples. And in other places we see that Jesus Himself offended the Pharisees because He broke their traditional rules by healing people on the Sabbath. From all of this we understand that Jesus felt meeting human needs and relieving suffering were more important than keeping a set of man-made rules. At the same time we know from His words in Matthew 5:17–18 that Jesus not only kept the Law but came to fulfill it. And in so doing He demonstrated His power and authority—*He* is the Lord of the Sabbath.

While the Pharisees of Jesus' day were nitpickers in their observance of the Sabbath, we seem to have gone to the other extreme. Not only have we, like the Pharisees, lost the spirit of the Sabbath, most of the other restraints have been cast aside as well.

As I reflected on this part of our lesson, I asked myself what we as individuals and as families can do to recover the true meaning and spirit of our Sabbath—Sunday. And here are some thoughts that have occurred to me.

To begin with, all of the preparation could, and probably should, be done before Sunday morning. This could include dinner planning and preparation, selecting and getting our clothes ready, and, above all, study and spiritual preparation for Sunday School and church. In fact, we might well take a lesson from our Jewish friends who begin their preparation on Friday night with a special family meal. Candles are lit, songs are sung, the children receive a blessing from their father, and the husband affirms love for his wife. It is a festive time when God is praised and the Torah is studied. Traditions and rituals are followed that have been handed down from generation to generation.

A suitable variation of this happy time could well serve as a model for us. We could start by setting aside Saturday night as a special time of Sunday preparation—a time of family togetherness and celebration accompanied by a specially prepared dinner. The evening around the table might be enriched by observing certain of the age-old traditions of our faith and the reading of Scripture. Each member of the family could participate, and a time might be set aside for sharing the blessings and experiences of the week. And this, of course, could be climaxed with a prayer time that would include everyone.

It is true that planning for such an evening each week needs to be carefully done so it is always a time of celebration as well as preparation for Sunday and worship in the Lord's house. And whether this special time of preparation includes one, two, or a half-dozen family members, it can and should be a time of anticipation.

So often, I wonder how many of God's blessings we miss because we aren't prepared to receive them—or we don't recognize them. Sunday is meant to be a day of blessing, of spiritual enrichment, of sharing with family and God's people in the joy of our salvation through Christ.

Jesus put it this way, "The sabbath was made for man, and not man for the sabbath."

LESSON 3
MARK 4:1–5:43

The Teacher Who Heals

Lord, help me to delight myself in Your Word. AMEN.

The synagogues were fast becoming closed to Jesus, so He began to teach by the sea. The crowd described in Chapter 4:1 was so large, "He entered into a ship, and sat in the sea; and the whole multitude was by the sea on the land." Jesus was a dynamic and dramatic teacher, not just a healer, as the crowd's response signifies.

In Chapter four we have Mark's largest single collection of Jesus' teachings. Jesus taught primarily in parables—a method very familiar to His Jewish listeners. By definition, a parable is a story used to illustrate a teaching by comparison, and the story is usually about a commonplace event. Jesus knew that His listeners were accustomed to thinking in pictures, and by using parables He could take abstract ideas and convert them into concrete and readily understandable truths.

We come now to Mark's account of Jesus' parable of the Sower and the four kinds of soil (4:3–9). Undoubtedly, from His vantage point in the boat that day, Jesus had a ringside view of a very familiar sight in first-century Palestine—a sower working in one of the fields near the seashore.

Building on this vivid picture, He pointed out that as the farmer sows his seed some of it falls on the hard-packed walkway along the edge of the field and is gobbled up by

The Sower and the soils.

birds. Other seed falls on rocky sections of the field where there is so little dirt, the seed can't really take root, and the little growth that does occur soon withers in the hot sun. Some of the seed inevitably lands in patches where thorns will eventually choke out any possible growth. But that seed which is sown on fertile, productive soil will produce a good harvest. He then concludes the story with this significant comment, "He that hath ears to hear, let him hear."

Next, we see that apparently the disciples were not clear as to His meaning, so in verses 14 through 20 Jesus carefully explains the meaning of the parable. The gist of the parable is being able to hear and comprehend Jesus' message. Mark's earliest readers knew that without a faith relationship to Jesus His teachings might not be clearly understood. But with a faith relationship the parable was a source of encouragement and hope—the kingdom of God had arrived with Jesus, and it is growing among us! From small beginnings come great endings.

The message for Mark's readers and us is, even though at times our witnessing to the gospel may seem to have little effect and may even appear to harden the hearts of those who hear it (4:12), the end result is in God's hands. We are responsible for our *faithfulness;* God is responsible for the *outcome.* Despite the unresponsiveness of some, and even the direct opposition of others, sharing the Good News of Jesus is a wonderful privilege.

This is a good passage to read if you feel discouraged over your efforts. Christians who find themselves spiritually dry, or congregations going through periods of sterility will profit from reading this parable. Nothing is quite so disheartening as having tried as hard as possible and exhausting every idea without any observable signs of progress. This is especially true in our success-oriented society. We want to be able to measure or chart results as we understand them.

Young pastors, full of enthusiasm and armed with the latest techniques, often go from seminary to small, sleepy, or dying churches. There they learn "the seven last words of the church": *We never did it that way before.* Unfortunately, these seven last words are descriptive of so much that goes on in churches, large or small. But our call as Christians is to be ever alert to every means and opportunity to share our faith. Our call as disciples of the Lord is to action, and our mission is to respond to the deep needs of people—

next door, in the neighborhood, across town in neglected areas, or any place in the world where there is suffering and ignorance.

At the same time we ought never to feel discouraged or defeated if our efforts are misunderstood or our words rejected. Again and again as we follow in the footsteps of Jesus through these Gospel lessons, we see Him misunderstood, not listened to, ignored, and even violently opposed. But that didn't stop Him. And that didn't stop Mark's earliest readers as they reflected on the truth of this parable. They had every cause to be discouraged because they were being persecuted for their faith. But the outcome of their lives was in the hands of God.

But the parable of the Sower and the soils does more than encourage the discouraged. It also challenges us: How good is *our* hearing? Jesus' words echo from the story as we seem to hear Him ask, "Do *you* hear me? Am I making myself clear?"

Let's look at Jesus' explanation of the story and interpret it for today. It is about four kinds of soil (hearers), and we may be more like the soil than the sower.

There are those who hear the message but reject it outright (4:15). The soil of their hearts is packed down and hard—the seed can't "take." In our experience, the gospel is often dismissed as irrelevant and impractical: "Love is a nice idea, but it won't work with the Communists"... "You can't be a Christian and make it in this dog-eat-dog, competitive world of business"... "If I'm nice to those kids, they'll take advantage of me." So often we clutch hard at old ideas and patterns and reject a new word or dismiss it as unworkable, simply because to accept it would call for us to change.

Then there are those hearers who receive the message but who do not persist in their faith (4:16). They have "no root in themselves, and so endure but for a time" (4:17). Among this type are those who see faith as an emotional high. It is a feeling, and as long as they feel good, all is well. But as soon as that "high" feeling sags, they give up.

Many young people—and older ones, too—have attended a church summer camp or retreat and made a commitment to Christ. They were uplifted and felt good while singing hymns on the lakeshore or around a campfire, and while surrounded by others who mirrored their enthusiasm.

But the test comes later when they return to their normal environments and routines. Unless their emotional high is buttressed by a persistence in faith, there is danger that the seed may not take root and grow.

Jesus refers next to a third kind of hearer (4:18–19). These are persons who are distracted by the temptations of the world. Jesus specifically lists three temptations. The temptation to become preoccupied with "the cares of this world," is mentioned first. This speaks of getting bogged down by the pressures of everyday life—earning a living, getting ahead, being socially accepted. Then, He refers to the temptation to concentrate on making money and acquiring material gain. And, third, having a "lust of other things"—anything that takes first place in our lives other than Jesus Christ. In other words, giving in to any of these temptations will choke out spiritual growth.

Fortunately, Jesus also reminds us that there are those who hear, receive, and act on the gospel message (4:20). These have ears to hear and listen with a third ear— the ear of faith. In a secular age like ours when people seem to find it so easy to ignore the message of Jesus Christ, the truth of this parable shouts to be heard and understood. In a culture that makes persistence in the Christian life difficult, the parable of the four kinds of soil speaks to our condition. It calls us to "hear the word, and receive it, and bring forth fruit."

It seems to me that this parable speaks pointedly to the necessity of spiritual growth. "Fruit-bearing Christians"— those whose lives reflect daily the Spirit of Christ—are involved in the work of the church, in prayer and fellowship with other Christians, in Bible study, and in ministering to the needs of their neighbors. This is our plan of action as we seek to grow and mature in our faith.

More parables.

In these next verses (4:21–25) Jesus stresses the importance of His teaching method and the way it is received. So important are the points He wants to make that He seems to be using different imagery to reemphasize what He has already said, to make sure we understand.

Jesus' parables are meant to be understood as surely as a torch or flashlight is meant to provide light. What may seem to be a riddle at first will eventually be explained or revealed. Both those who understand and those who do not are encourged to keep listening: "For there is nothing hid, which shall not be manifested; neither was anything kept secret, but that it should come about. If any man has ears to hear, let him hear" (4:22–23).

Jesus obviously understood a point that authorities in communications stress today. Seeing and hearing are alike in the sense that both depend on the faculty of receiving. The kind of hearing Jesus is referring to is really "listening." We don't necessarily "receive" everything we hear. But listening is an active exercise; it demands attention and concentration. There is a two-way responsibility if communication is to be effective. It calls for a clear "sender" and an attentive "receiver."

Our experience verifies this insight. Most college students learn to comprehend material as they move from their freshman to senior years. As one woman put it, after having taken a course in her senior year from a teacher she had found boring in a freshman class, "It was amazing how much better the teacher had become in only three years." Probably the student—the hearer—had grown in her ability to receive ideas.

In other words, Jesus is telling us that listening is serious business. It is a gift that can be cultivated. "Active listening" is taught in some places, and the program is built upon the premise that we can learn to hear both ideas and emotions. Failure to listen carefully can become a habit that feeds on itself. The more carefully we give attention to the Word of God, the more profound its message becomes (4:24–25). If we don't use the gift of listening we lose it— we lose the ability to *receive ideas*—they go "in one ear and out the other."

Jesus never felt that everyone who heard His message would understand, much less respond. As persuasive as He was, we are free moral agents and we may listen—or not. It is up to us.

This particular parable of the seed that grows while the sower is asleep (4:26–29) is, in a way, an extension of or an elaboration on the parable of the Sower and the four kinds of soil. In the story of the Sower and the soils we have a picture of God, the Sower; and people, the soil, acting together to bring about God's kingdom.

Now Jesus gives us this second parable to emphasize

The power of small beginnings.

the truth that it is God's supernatural action that makes spiritual growth possible. The story shows that God has made a world in which seeds that are planted grow, and the results do not depend on human effort.

Many worthwhile enterprises demonstrate this truth. Abraham Lincoln was shocked and dismayed when, as a young man, he first saw people being sold like cattle. A sense of the injustice of slavery grew like a seed within him, and his full-grown response as president changed history.

And Christianity began as a tiny, seemingly trivial movement. It appeared to be just one more pathetic sect that was doomed to eventual extinction. When contrasted with the military and material might of the powerful Roman Empire, it seemed to have no chance. Yet the empire that Pilate and Herod represented came to an end, while the small fellowship of Christians not only endured, but transformed the world. It was God's power to change the hearts and wills of people that made the difference then. And it is that same power at work in our twentieth-century world that changes people from being hesitant human beings into bold forces for good and for God.

In the parable of the mustard seed (4:30–32) Jesus tells us how the world is really changed. It is not remade by external forces but by seeds that are planted—ideas and movements that have the power to convince people and change lives. And the word picture He gives us to illustrate this is the smallest of seeds, yet when these seeds sprout and grow, they become towering and useful trees. Surely the growth of the Church Universal from its small beginnings in that little tension-wracked country in the first century, to what it has become today, may well be the greatest miracle of all.

Small beginnings remind Christians, also, to not take themselves too seriously. Some groups pride themselves on smallness. They have small beginnings, and, unfortunately, they experience small ends as well. One tiny church group in its annual report commented that "while it had lost several members over the past year, those who remained were as faithful as ever."

The parable of the mustard seed underlines the truth for us that the size of any of our beginnings is not particularly important. Instead, it is God's presence and power that enables a seed to grow and bear fruit. Without God's participation, and in spite of our best efforts, ideas curdle and movements die.

Jesus had been teaching by the seashore all day. Now, when evening came, He sent the crowds home, and Jesus and His disciples got into a boat and started across the Sea of Galilee. Mark gives us next the story of what happened when a violent storm caught them out in the middle of the sea (4:35–41).

On the surface this seems to be entirely different material from what went on before in chapter four. Until this incident is reported, Mark is calling attention to Jesus' teaching in parables and the importance of hearing and understanding. Calming the sea appears to be out of context with the rest of the chapter.

Not so. As we continue the story, Mark tells us that when the storm struck, Jesus was asleep in the bow of the boat, not the least bit concerned about anything that might happen. But as the wind and the waves beat on the boat, the disciples panicked. They awakened Jesus with the question, "Master, carest thou not that we perish?" Their question indicates that while they had been "hearing" Him all day long, they hadn't been "listening." His words throughout the day had stressed the power of God in all kinds of situations, but now they were paralyzed with fear because they hadn't really listened and understood what He had been saying.

Jesus' command, "Peace, be still," which silences the storm, is evidence of His authority. Jesus says to His frightened disciples, "Why are ye so fearful? how is it that ye have no faith?" (4:40). His question implies amazement. All day Jesus had been teaching about the importance of hearing God's word about hope and trust, and the first storm they face frightens the disciples clear out of their sandals.

Mark's first-century readers would have found another level of meaning in this episode. A storm-tossed boat with Jesus in it was an accurate symbol of their historical circumstances. They were continually facing persecution, and this event reminded them that Jesus, Lord of history, was still in control. It was intended to reassure them, for they, too, were asking: "Master, carest thou not that we perish?" (4:38). Jesus' answer is simply, "Trust me."

Calming the storm.

Calming the sea is a story that also speaks to our condition. As individuals, we hear that God is One in whom we can put our trust, but trusting is not always easy when the "waters are rough." Jesus was with the disciples, and still they were afraid. Jesus is with us, too, and our lives are often fraught with anxiety. What is our answer? Again, I believe we have our answer as the Word of God takes root and grows in our lives—as we not only hear but actively listen to what He is saying to us—and we really come to know through experience that nothing can come between us and the love of God.

Calming demons—Jesus and the Gadarene demoniac.

After Jesus muzzled the storm and calmed the sea, He and the disciples continued across the Sea of Galilee to its southeastern shore. This was a relatively remote area inhabited largely by gentiles. No sooner did they land in the country of the Gadarenes than Jesus was challenged to calm another storm—this time in a man whose mind had gone out of control (5:1–19). Mark describes him as having "an unclean spirit," and says the man was living among the tombs.

The creature who confronted Jesus was more monster than man: "No man could bind him, no, not with chains, because that he had been often bound with fetters and chains, and the chains had been plucked asunder by him, and the fetters broken in pieces; neither could any man tame him" (5:3–4). In many respects it is difficult for us today to identify with this scene. However, it was a familiar one to the people of Jesus' day. On the other hand, anyone who has worked in the more violent sections of a mental hospital or who has attempted to control a person overdosed on certain drugs will agree that Mark's description is not farfetched. Insane people provoke in others feelings of both pity and fear. And, certainly, both elements are present in this eerie story.

It seems clear from the words and actions of the man that the demons were in complete control. In fact, he was so under the control of the demons that at times he seems to be speaking while at other times the demons are speaking through him. But as desperate as his condition was, it would appear that this poor man had become comfortable with his condition because he asks Jesus to let him alone (5:7).

However, as strange as this setting is to us, there is an

Gadara and the cliff-like slopes leading down to the Sea of Galilee. According to some traditions, this is the setting for the story of the healing of the Gadarene demoniac and the rushing of the demon-possessed swine down these slopes into the waters of the Sea of Galilee.

important lesson for our times. The evil that lies behind the demoniac is just as destructive today as it was in Jesus' day even though it takes different forms. But the power of Christ provides the answer now even as it did then.

Next, we see Jesus dealing with the deranged man by attacking the trouble at its evil source, "For he said unto him, Come out of the man, thou unclean spirit" (5:8). Then Jesus spoke again and asked, "What is thy name?" And the response came, "My name is Legion: for we are many" (5:9). This answer gives us a vivid word picture of the multitudes of demons that were in control of this frantic and desperate man.

With an authoritative command, Jesus then instructed the demons to leave the man and enter a herd of swine, which were grazing nearby, "...and the herd ran violently down a steep place into the sea (there were about two thousand swine) and were choked in the sea" (5:13).

The swineherders reacted to their loss by demanding

that Jesus leave. They did this partly out of fear and partly out of resentment over the destruction of their property. Their reaction, ironically, is like the first response of the demon-possessed man—they didn't want to be disturbed by Jesus either. Jesus represented a threat to the way things were, and no *status quo* is safe from the Great Disturber. We would think that they should have been happy over the man's miraculous healing, but instead they were more concerned about the loss of their pigs.

So Jesus left. Here, as we've seen elsewhere, Jesus does not force Himself on people. He honors our freedom to receive or reject Him because He knows that those who don't want help will not receive it. The healed man, however, is a different story. The contrast between the man possessed and the man cured is dramatic. The language of conversion is appropriate for describing the change: he was born again. He was transformed. He was a brand-new human being.

Understandably, he wanted to join Jesus and the disciples. He wanted to sustain contact with the One who had made him whole, but that was not what Jesus had in mind. "Go home to thy friends," Jesus said, "and tell them how great things the Lord hath done for thee, and hath had compassion on thee" (5:19). Jesus knew that this man's life validated His message, for all those who had known him as insane would come to know him as whole—and learn the reason why. At this point, a gentile could best minister to gentiles.

The calling of the demon-possessed man is instructive for the rest of us. "Before" and "after" conversion experiences are effective witnesses when they are tested day-to-day among friends and acquaintances. If our attitudes, behavior, and life-styles are constantly different, so much so that the hometown folks are impressed, a conversion experience is completed. We may be able to convince strangers rather easily that we were once lost but now are saved. But with the people next door and down the street, the standard is higher, and, therefore, the authenticity of the conversion is more powerful.

It is sometimes easier to go to a distant place to serve God, but Jesus often calls us to stay home and minister where we are. Mark reports (5:20) that the man "began to publish in Decapolis how great things Jesus had done for him; and *all men did marvel*" (italics mine).

When Jesus and the disciples returned by boat to the Galilean side, a familiar scene greeted them. Crowds swarmed on the shore even before the boat was docked. Mark then blends two stories together. The story of a sick woman (5:25–34) is sandwiched between the beginning and ending of the story about the healing of Jairus' daughter (5:22–24, 35–43).

Mark's Gospel again exhibits the ring of truth. One could hardly expect crowds of sick and hurting people to wait in orderly lines, like bakery customers who take a number and wait to be called. We would expect them to get in each other's way and compete for Jesus' time and attention.

And this is exactly what happened. Jesus is presented with an emergency while He is on His way to an emergency. Jairus, a ruler of the synagogue, has come to Jesus in desperation, begging Him to heal his young daughter. We can be sure this was a dangerous step for Jairus to take, as he was opening himself up to public embarrassment and ridicule for kneeling at Jesus' feet. The ever-present Pharisees most likely noted his desperate actions and would surely use them against him.

Yet, Jairus' action was true-to-life. Even a stubborn synagogue ruler will set aside his prejudices when his daughter's life is at stake. The drama of the situation could have been made for television: Will Jesus get there in time? And the tension is increased when His journey is interrupted by another person seeking help.

The way Jesus deals with interruptions is noteworthy. A little girl is dying, yet Jesus stops to ask a question His own disciples think is absurd. Busy Christians will recognize His dilemma. We are continually beset by new needs while in the process of dealing with old ones. So often we confront suffering on the way to the hospital. But I think one of the hardest lessons for any of us to learn is that when it comes to meeting human need, there aren't such things as interruptions—only opportunities to help and serve.

A woman approaches Jesus from out of the crowd. She has a blood disease—possibly some form of menstrual problem that would have made her ritually unclean as well as physically ill. Mark says she had been ill for twelve years, and "she had suffered many things of many physicians, and had spent all that she had, and was nothing

A story within a story.

55

bettered, but rather grew worse" (5:28). And to make matters worse, it had been necessary during all of that time for her to have no physical contact with another person (Lev. 15:25–27). She had actually broken the Law by touching the fringe of Jesus' robe.

Her hope is clearly stated by Mark, "For she said, if I may touch but his clothes, I shall be whole" (5:28). In spite of the crowd pressing about Him as He walked along, Jesus is aware of the woman's touch. Mark differentiates between "thronging," (5:31) which means to jostle, push, or rub shoulders with Jesus as it were; and "touching," which is what the woman did, and which Jesus immediately recognized as more than just physical proximity (5:30). The crowd and Jesus' disciples, however, could not tell the difference.

But there is a vital difference. The crowd has casual contact with Jesus. It is purposeless, accidental. The woman approaches Jesus with hope and expectation, and she is rewarded by being healed. The crowd pressing about Jesus may have been along for the stroll, curious to see if Jesus could pull off another miracle—this time in Jairus' home. But the woman wanted to "touch" Jesus as an act of faith, hoping He might heal her.

She demonstrated great personal integrity, too. When Jesus called for the one who had "touched" His clothes to come forward, she did so "fearing and trembling." She could have slipped away and remained anonymous, but she took a risk (after all, she had broken the Law) and was rewarded. Not only was she healed, but Jesus gave her His blessing, "Daughter, thy faith hath made thee whole; go in peace, and be whole of thy plague" (5:34). As he had done before with others, Jesus made possible her re-entry into society. He had declared her clean and given her a new outlook on life. Jesus showed that God's purpose is to make people whole again, which is what "being saved" really means.

Modern men and women can profit from reflecting on the nature of this woman's faith. We may be tempted to disdain the naive form her faith took—wanting, as she did, simply to touch His garments in order to be healed. At one level the story suggests superstition or, at best, a simple-minded understanding of faith healing.

That is why a careful reading of the text is necessary. Her initial contact with Jesus was an act of desperation. All other attempts for healing had failed. However, Jesus' reaction to her coming out of the crowd was significant. She became more than a spectator, and she rose above her fears and "told him all the truth" (5:33). What "all the truth" included we cannot know. But it is safe to assume that she poured out feelings of rejection, loneliness, despair, and pain. She may have expected a "quickie" healing and discovered that personal hands-on contact with Jesus brought more. It made "wholeness"—salvation—possible.

This is why truly effective evangelists do more than just call people to the altar. A Billy Graham crusade uses hundreds of personal counselors and prayer-partners because the experience of salvation involves concern for physical, mental, and spiritual needs—the whole person. The modern-day Salvation Army does more than preach sermons and provide soup kitchens. It treats the diseases of alcoholism and malnutrition. Churches that respond to a variety of human conditions become involved in mental health programs as well as preaching missions. And well they should, for out of the crowd may come desperate, hurting persons who need Christ's wholistic healing.

"While he yet spake," writes Mark, "there came from the ruler of the synagogue's house messengers which said, 'Thy daughter is dead; why troublest thou the Master any further?'" (5:35). The interruption along the way had taken too long. Jesus didn't arrive in time. Why go on with this business? There's no more hope!

Meanwhile, back on the road.

Jesus' response sounds much like His words to the disciples when He calmed the sea, "Be not afraid, only believe" (5:36). Then, taking only His most trusted disciples, Peter, James, and John, Jesus went to the house where the ruler of the synagogue lived. The scene He found there was chaotic by our standards, although it was typical of what happened during Jewish mourning. Mourners wailed, tore their hair, beat their breasts, and ripped their clothing. The contrast Mark draws is obvious: the scene of confusion and despair, and Jesus' words of comfort, "Be not afraid."

Jesus' statement, "The damsel is not dead but sleepeth," was greeted by scornful laughter and loud guffaws. So He cleared the room, except for the little girl's parents, and brings her back to life. Mark's readers understood: death is like sleep; it can be reversed in the resurrection. The word to the little girl was a word for all followers of Jesus.

The personal, intimate quality that Jesus' ministry often demonstrated is captured in this healing. "Talitha, cumi" can be translated "Little lamb, arise" (5:41). Jesus could be tough on the Pharisees, intimidating to demons, yet tender with children.

Mark's interest in detail appears again, as he reports that Jesus "commanded that something should be given her to eat" (5:45). Again, Jesus ministers to the whole person. The child had been ill and she needed food to get her strength back.

The story ends with an unanswered question. Surely it occurred to Jesus that the raising of the synagogue ruler's daughter might have significant implications. If Jairus were won over to Jesus' following, think of the potential for other converts. In contrast to what He told the demon-possessed man living in the country of the Gadarenes, Jesus instructed the few eyewitnesses to this miracle to say nothing to anyone. In our slang we might say that Jesus refused to take a "cheap shot." He could have exploited the circumstances to promote His own cause among the scribes and Pharisees. That He chose not to do so indicates His unwillingness to manipulate or pressure people into the Kingdom.

The power and authority of Jesus are implied in the parables of Mark. The Kingdom of God has begun to be seen, heard, and experienced in the presence of Jesus. Yet, it is grasped by only a few and misunderstood by most. The "secret" of who Jesus is continues to be revealed but not all have ears to hear or eyes to see.

Mark also shows that what Jesus teaches is linked to what He does. Jesus tells us to trust Him and not be afraid. His words are undergirded by what happens when He enters our turmoil: a turbulent sea is calmed; a bedeviled man is liberated; a chronically ill woman is healed; a dead child is made alive. And Jesus, the teacher, also brings us peace.

Lord, let the seed of this lesson fall on good soil and reap a fruitful harvest in my life. AMEN.

WHAT THIS SCRIPTURE MEANS TO ME—Mark 4:1—5:43

One of my college roommates spent a summer on a ship in the waters off Alaska. Joyce was working as a part of a team for a mission board doing Vacation Bible Schools at small port towns that had "circuit riding preachers" stop by once or twice a month. The team would be dropped off to do a Bible School and then be picked up a week later and taken on to the next port. It sounded terribly exciting and romantic to me, for I was from Tucson, Arizona, which is in the hot and arid Sonoran desert.

One day, Dottie, a mutual friend, called me and asked, "Patty, have you heard from Joyce in the last few days?"

"No, why?" I asked.

"They're afraid the ship Joyce is on is lost at sea!"

"Oh, no! Why do they think that?"

"Well, they haven't been heard from for over a week. They've been in radio contact weekly with the Southern California mission headquarters, but their call didn't come in this week, and they can't be reached! There's a terrible storm off the coast of Alaska, in the area where they are supposed to be. Russ called to ask us to pray." (Russ was Joyce's fiance.)

"Oh, wow! Of course, I'll pray, but call me as soon as you know anything."

A few days later, Dottie called back:

"Praise the Lord! They are all safe! They made it through the storm!"

When we all got back to college in the fall, we inundated Joyce with questions about what happened. This is her story:

"We were picked up from the small port town on the west coast of Alaska, not far from Anchorage, and headed out to sea enroute to the Kodiak area. After several hours, the sky got black and the winds started howling. It wasn't long before the waves were crashing over the ship, tossing it around like a toy in a bathtub. Boy, was it scary!

"The ship's crew ordered us to go below deck and stay there. The storm raged for several days with the ship being buffeted about by gale-force winds, and we were lashed by driving sheets of rain. Only a few crew members were allowed on deck, and they had to be secured with lines.

"Almost everyone was sick and couldn't keep any food down. It was a mess. I tried to cheer everybody up, but I admit I was scared, too.

"After several days the storm ended as abruptly as it had started. The wind had driven us way off course, but we finally made it to our next port. What an experience! I hope I never go through another storm like that in my life."

This experience of Joyce's helps me better understand the story in our lesson where we read about a trip Jesus and His disciples took across the Sea of Galilee. Evidently it was calm when they started out, but as can happen there even today, a violent storm swooped down from the surrounding mountains. Their boat was caught right in the middle of it, and the disciples were terror-stricken. While they were accustomed to the storms that hit Galilee, evidently this was the worst they had experienced, for Mark tells us that they awakened Jesus who was asleep in the back of the boat and shouted, "Master, carest thou not that we perish?" Of course He cared, and with a word He rebuked the wind and it stopped.

During my teenage years I invited Jesus to come on board my "life-ship," and He did. Together we've weathered some frightful storms, and there have been times when I thought He must be asleep. In such moments I would cry out in desperation for Him to take over the helm of my life and steer us to safety. Then there have been other times when in my calm life-seas that I've taken matters into my own hands and have replaced Him at the helm. But then the minute the seas got rough I would want Him to take over again.

I'm sure this is a common experience with all of us. One would think we would learn to always let Him, through guidance, keep the helm of our lives and do the steering. But somehow we seem to have a penchant for "taking over," and when we do, things get rough.

Sometimes when that happens I cry out like the disciples did that night, "Master, don't you care that I am dying?" But then He rebukes the storm, turns to me and seems to say, "Oh, you of little faith! Why are you so afraid? I'm here with you."

With that, I'm reminded just how often Jesus has come to me in the middle of my struggles with the words, "Peace be still." Whenever that happens, a great calm settles down over me. And then I feel a sense of awe as the realization comes again that even "the wind and the sea obey Him." This Savior of ours will always hold us steady through all of our "storms" if we let Him.

LESSON 4
MARK 6:1–8:26

The Struggle to Know Jesus

Lord, with this lesson, give me an understanding of Your Word. AMEN.

Just a little over a year had passed since Jesus first left Nazareth and traveled down the east side of the Jordan River to be baptized by John at Bethany beyond Jordan. Mark has taken us through this time with almost breakneck speed. We have seen Jesus begin His ministry in Galilee and select His twelve disciples, and then move on to preach, teach, and heal the sick.

Out of all that happened during that year, Mark has described for us the healing of the man with an unclean spirit in the Capernaum synagogue, the curing of Simon Peter's mother-in-law, and the healing of the man sick with palsy. We have watched Jesus as He boldly defied the Pharisees in the synagogue and healed the man with a withered hand, as He stopped the storm on the Sea of Galilee with His word, and in the country of the Gadarenes as He commanded the demons to leave the man. Through Mark's eyes we followed Jesus as He healed the hemorrhaging woman who had mustered up nerve enough to reach out and touch the hem of His robe on a crowded street while He was on His way to give life back to Jairus' daughter. In addition, Mark tells us again and again that He healed many people who crowded around Him and appealed for His help.

At this stage of His ministry Jesus was enthusiastically

Jesus visits His hometown.

61

A street scene in Nazareth where Jesus grew up into young manhood. It was the people here who knew Him only as "the carpenter, the son of Mary."

received wherever He went. So now, as He headed back to His hometown of Nazareth, for the first time since He'd left, Jesus had every reason to believe He would be received joyfully (6:1–6).

But such was not the case. First we read that Jesus' friends and relatives were astonished at His teaching, and then they were offended by Him (6:3). They saw Jesus merely as a carpenter, a working man turned rabbi, and they rejected anything He had to say. Jesus was too ordinary to be the Messiah, and no person seems more ordinary than when he returns to his boyhood home. They saw Him only as "the son of Mary, the brother of James, and Joseph, and of Juda, and Simon." This reference to Jesus as "the son of Mary" could have two possible meanings: Joseph His father was dead, or it may have been an insolent reference to His dubious parentage.

Their rejection of Him was so complete that He could do no mighty work there, so He left. From this point on we see a dramatic change in His approach. It was the custom of traveling rabbis to visit and teach in the synagogues wherever they went. However, because of the bitter contention that had accompanied all such visits up to this time, Jesus discontinued the practice. Instead, He now began ministering to people on hillsides, along the seashore, or from fishing boats.

The rejection of Jesus at Nazareth convinced Him of the need for a new strategy of outreach. He moved now to multiply His ministry by sending forth His disciples. We have seen how He called them (1:16–20), and Mark later identifies all the disciples by name (3:13–19). Now, Jesus sends them out "by two and two; and gave them power over unclean spirits" (6:7). Their instructions were simple but direct: travel light. Their mission was urgent, and they would have to rely on the power of God, not the signs and symbols of wealth and status.

A new strategy.

No longer could the disciples be merely learners at the feet of Jesus. They had been His students for over a year. Now they were to become emissaries, and they were to take nothing with them except what was essential: Christ's authority and power. Jesus knew from experience that the material "stuff" of the world tends to negate effective ministry. The wealthier those who proclaim the gospel become, the more their proclamation may be discredited. Doing good and doing well are often contradictory.

The same is true today. Preachers and evangelists may well lose credibility when their financial successes are revealed. In contrast, each generation is inspired by the story of an Albert Schweitzer who abandoned several distinguished careers to go to Africa as a medical missionary, or a Mother Teresa who dedicates her life to the poor and dying.

As Jesus sent out His disciples, He told them to remain centered on the main task. He also advised them to accept whatever hospitality that was offered to them, and to not wait around for a better deal.

If people refused to listen to them and turned them

away, as Jesus' friends and relatives had done to Him, they were simply to move on and continue the task. It was not their role to be argumentative or contentious. Their sole commission was to preach the Good News about Jesus and to exercise their God-given power to heal the sick and cast out demons.

We, too, can heed Jesus' counsel. This passage (6:11) teaches us how to handle failure. Don't persist in lost causes. Shake off the dust, move on to the next place, and leave the judgment to God. This verse also tells us that as Christ's disciples and witnesses today, we are not responsible for the results of our sharing, since only God can determine the outcome. But we are responsible for our *obedience.*

Meanwhile, back at the palace.

Mark 6:14–29 represents a kind of flashback to a birthday feast in the palace of Herod Antipas, the son of Herod the Great. The only previous reference to it was in 1:14 when, quite without warning, we were informed that John the Baptist had been put into prison.

The news of Jesus as teacher and healer had finally reached Herod. Mark suggests that Herod's superstitious fear, exaggerated by a bad conscience, convinced him that John the Baptist had risen from the dead (6:16). Guilt's hobgoblins evidently tormented Herod.

A considerable amount of background information about Herod is available to us, some of which is implied in these verses. Life in his court was immoral and unrestrained. Herod Antipas had married Herodias, the former wife of his half brother Philip. And John the Baptist had boldly condemned this bit of wife-swapping, "For John had said unto Herod, It is not lawful for thee to have thy brother's wife" (6:18). The king, oddly, was ambivalent in his response to John the Baptist. Having thrown John into prison at his fortress of Machaerus, Herod would from time to time bring him out, for he knew John was a good and just man. Mark credits Herod with recognizing John's virtue, even though Herod had been denounced by John.

Herod's mistress-wife, Herodias, had no such scruples, however. She was determined to protect her position as Herod's spouse, even if Jewish law forbad it (Lev. 18:16; 20:21). So Mark reports the well-known story of how the daughter of Herodias, identified elsewhere as Salome, danced so well at Herod's birthday party, that he offered to give her anything she wanted. After a quick consultation with her mother, she requested the head of John the Baptist be brought to her on a platter (6:24–25).

Herod was trapped by his drunken promise. His good intentions—to hear John's word—were lost in the fallout of his posturing: "And the king was exceedingly sorry; yet for his oath's sake, and for their sakes which sat with him, he would not reject her" (6:26).

So John became a victim, a martyr to prophetic courage, and a casualty of Herodias' revenge. The early readers of Mark's Gospel would have seen in this story a foreshadowing of the death of Jesus. In Mark's description of the court of Herod, it was clear that flickering good intentions were smothered by fear, envy, and ambition. The followers of Jesus in any era should note this and take heed. Those who trust in politics and power to protect them will be disappointed, and compromise with such forces is impossible. The early Christians, many facing martyrdom themselves, would have understood.

The feeding of the 5,000 is the only miracle of Jesus reported in all four Gospels. Clearly the event was not anticipated; it simply happened. Mark tells us that Jesus had had a private retreat with His disciples in mind: "And he said unto them, 'Come ye yourselves apart into a desert place, and rest awhile': for there were many coming and going, and they had no leisure so much as to eat" (6:31).

The feeding of the 5,000.

These words are certainly reminiscent of the way most of us live today. Our lives are so jammed with activity and our minds are so filled with routine clutter that it is easy to lose touch with ourselves and with God. And while it doesn't come easy, we must, at frequent intervals, schedule times of quiet and rest for ourselves if we are to be at our creative best. It is in our quiet times, our rest times, that we are best able to hear the voice of God.

Jesus understood the need for this all too well, but this time it was not to be. Crowds of people saw them leaving and hurried on ahead. The King James Bible describes their eagerness to be with Jesus in quaint language, "(They) ran afoot thither out of all cities, and outwent them, and came together unto him" (6:33). Having been "outwented," Jesus was moved by compassion and ministered to them. He saw them as "sheep without a shepherd," and He taught them.

So purposeful was Jesus with His teaching that He completely forgot the crowd's physical hunger. The disciples had to interrupt and remind Him that they had missed lunch. Then what happened next has been thought about and discussed for centuries. Mark says Jesus took five loaves of bread and two fish, blessed them, and then had the disciples distribute the food among the crowd.

Some readers understand this symbolically, as a form of holy communion. They see it as a celebration, an experience of worship. Others say that Jesus' example inspired the crowd to share the food they had brought for themselves, and this made it possible for everyone to have something to eat. And the most obvious reading of the text is to take it at face value. Jesus took the five small loaves and the two fish and miraculously caused them to be multiplied.

As we look back at the story, we're told that the disciples' growling stomachs reminded them it was long past time to eat. Jesus had been teaching them, but now He modeled what is characteristic of the gospel: He was concerned with their physical needs. Christianity is not simply a spiritual religion. Jesus' compassion included both spiritual and physical food. And Christian concern is for both bodies and souls. We are called to build hospitals *and* churches, to provide medicine for those who need it, to feed the hungry, *and* to nourish the spiritually deprived.

But as the disciples saw the problem, they confronted it realistically. It was late and the only sensible thing to do was to disperse the crowd and send them away to find food. But Jesus had another idea. "You give them something to eat." They were flabbergasted, and their frustration shows in their reply, "Shall we go and buy two hundred pennyworth of bread, and give them to eat?" (6:37). That would have been close to a year's pay—and there were no credit cards!

This is where the incident speaks to us. As we look around at the needs of the world, we are overwhelmed. Our inadequacies leap out at us, and it seems hopeless. Like our predecessors, Jesus' disciples, we protest that too much is expected of us, and when we take inventory, our worst fears are justified. Compared to the world's needs, our resources are pathetic. What difference does it make how many loaves we have? There isn't enough to feed the crowd. Our inventory, like the disciples', sounds like Mother Hubbard at her cupboard.

But wait just a moment! Remember Gideon and his little army of three hundred men, David and Goliath, Paul in Ephesus, Schweitzer in Lambarene, Martin Luther King in Montgomery? All odds were against them, but they got it done. Five thousand hungry people? Five little loaves and two fish? Preposterous! But Jesus managed it. The people ate all they could and there was food left over.

Our curiosity drives us to ask how Jesus did it, but that's really not important. Mark wants us to see the *people,* not the loaves and the fish. He reminds his readers and us that five loaves and two fish are plenty because Christ will make them sufficient. You and I can face the world with our little bits and not panic because Christ, with His blessing, can make them adequate.

We all feel inadequate in the face of the world's material and spiritual needs. Yet, again and again, Christ performs miracles through concerned people. Not long ago I read a story about a young student minister who had visited one day with a very sick patient. Later, the patient told the hospital chaplain that the young man's visit had been crucial to his recovery—the words spoken and the prayer offered brought hope and life at a time of deep need. The patient never saw the young man again, and that student minister probably never knew how God had used his visit that day. Christ had blessed that student's "loaves" and a needy patient had been fed in spite of human inadequacy.

Walking on water.

That Mark places the story of Jesus' walking on the sea right after the feeding of the five thousand is significant (6:47–52). The phrase "walking on water" has become part of our vocabulary and it means now what it meant then: doing something incredible. Mark is telling us that the disciples could not make connections between the feeding of the five thousand and Jesus' coming to meet them on the water: "And he went up unto them into the ship; and the wind ceased: and they were sore amazed in themselves beyond measure, and wondered. For they considered not the miracle of the loaves: for their heart was hardened" (6:51–52).

The incredible act of miraculous feeding was forgotten as soon as the disciples, floundering in the wind-tossed boat enroute to Bethsaida, found themselves once again in trouble. When Jesus came walking toward them on the water, He was not at first perceived as a comforting presence, but as some sort of ghost (6:49). It was only after He spoke to them and calmed the wind that they recognized Him: "And immediately he talked with them, and saith unto them, be of good cheer; it is I; be not afraid" (6:50).

Once again, the earliest readers of Mark's Gospel would have seen themselves in this story. St. Augustine articulated Mark's subliminal message: "He came treading the waves; and so He puts all the swelling tumults of life under His feet. Christians—why be afraid?"

These verses hint at one of the most perplexing problems of communication that we Christians face. To the question, how do we survive the truly difficult storms of life? the Christian answer is: because Christ is with us. But at times when we are experiencing excruciating stress, that answer may seem inadequate unless we remember and relive those earlier moments when Christ's presence and power overcame our fears and calmed our internal and external storms. In recalling this vivid story of Christ's presence on the wind-driven sea during those black early morning hours when the disciples were straining against fearsome odds, Mark wants his readers and us to remember that we're never alone. To remember those earlier acts of His saving grace is to receive strength for present difficulties.

Later when the boat landed on the shores of Gennesaret, a familiar scene was repeated. Crowds of sick, hurting people thronged around Jesus. The able-bodied carried bedridden persons to Him: "They laid the sick in the streets and besought him that they might touch if it were but the border of his garments" (6:56).

Jesus feeds the hungry, walks on water, heals the sick. In fact, we're told that all who "touched him were made whole." Mark's point fairly screams at his readers: Do you not see who Jesus is? And the answer, sadly enough, is that many still do not comprehend or understand that the Messiah, the world's Savior, has come to deliver people from the sickness and oppression of sin.

Denouncing the Pharisees.   Immediately following these peak experiences, the chief adversaries of Jesus reappeared on the scene and instigated the sixth controversy between Jesus and the religious authorities, which Mark records in his Gospel. This time the issue centered around external requirements of the Law and scribal traditions.

A swat team of scribes and Pharisees from Jerusalem confronted Him about a picky tradition deeply rooted in Jewish Oral Law that applied to the ritual of washing hands before eating "...when they saw some of his disciples eat bread with defiled, that is to say, with unwashen hands, they found fault" (7:2).

The issue at stake had nothing to do with hygiene but with ceremonial cleansing. Several hundred years earlier, the scribes had set out to implement the moral rules set down in the Pentateuch, and in time, literally thousands of small laws were established to regulate all of Jewish life. These became known as the "tradition of the elders" (7:5). Ceremonial handwashing was among these rules. The demands were ridiculous—the water used had to be kept in certain types of containers. The hands had to be held in a certain position for washing. There was a specific way in which the water was to be poured over the hands. There were rules for every step, and there were a lot of steps.

These meaningless man-made rules were what Jesus' disciples failed to keep. But in the critical eyes of the Pharisees the breaking of these rules was an affront to God. Tragically, this tradition of faultfinding has pervaded the church from then until now. To stress man-made rules and laws and codes of behavior is to negate the spirit of Christ just as much today as when the Pharisees found fault with the disciples.

On the other hand, Jesus stressed that all ceremonies are created by people. People, not God, make cups and the rules about handling cups (7:8). Rituals are externals. Jesus does not say externals are evil, but His point is that internal reality is crucial. If we have the proper inner motivation, for example, love for others; and a proper relationship with God, for example, commitment to Him; external rules are unnecessary. Proper ceremonial washing isn't needed if, so to speak, our hands are clean before God. And if they are not clean before God, all the scrubbing in the world will do no good. Jesus shows that real blasphemy comes from deifying the trivial.

Jesus' response to the carping of His critics has the ring of an Old Testament prophet. In fact, He quotes Isaiah in Mark 7:6, "This people honoureth me with their lips, but their heart is far from me." To further emphasize His point, "...ye reject the commandment of God, that ye may keep your own tradition" (7:9), Jesus discusses using the custom of Corban. The practice of Corban meant that a son could set aside a material possession as a gift for holy use sometime in the future (7:10–13). The son might then justify neglect for his needy parents, even though he had the means to help them. It would be like our refusing to help our needy parents, even though we had money in long-term certificates of deposit, because there was a penalty for early withdrawal. People of any era who really care for parents will set aside man-made traditions in the name of love. Jesus saw Corban as a way of evading a fundamental duty to honor parents. The custom was strangling the intent of the commandment. At the same time, Jesus was speaking out against religious forms and practices that place a higher priority on laws and rules than on meeting the needs of people. Our role as Christians is to love, not find fault or become slaves to legalities.

Back to reality.   Jesus' argument about inner and outer religion makes good sense, and it is a striking contrast to the petty legalism of His opponents. From the perspective of the Pharisees, however, Jesus was performing radical moral surgery. In Chapter seven Mark reports two more healings that also demonstrated Jesus' break with the past. Just as He had declared all foods clean regardless of ceremony, in these stories He insists that all persons are clean. First, He casts out a demon from the daughter of a Syrophoenecian woman (7:24–30), and later He heals a gentile deaf man near Decapolis (7:31–37). Mark's readers would have seen in both events a continuing repudiation by Jesus of long-standing taboos.

Jesus and His disciples had left Capernaum and traveled the forty to fifty miles to Phoenicia and the region of Tyre and Sidon—gentile territory. Possibly they were seeking temporary relief from the harassment of the scribes and Pharisees. At any rate, when the Syrophoenician woman found Jesus, she ran the risk of being rejected or humiliated. Since she was Greek, her ethnic identity was a barrier to Jews, and it was like our asking for help from someone we didn't know personally, and everything we did know—of their race, religion, and custom—was negative. On the surface, Jesus' reply to her plea to "cast forth the devil out of her daughter" seems flippant: "Let the children first be filled: for it is not meet to take the children's bread, and to cast it unto the dogs" (7:27).

His words meant that He must first feed the Jews (children) and not gentiles (dogs). Was He being cruel and insensitive? Not at all. The probability is that Jesus was bantering with the woman, the way in which people of different races sometimes joke about visible racial differences that separate them. And it seems to me that the idea that Jesus was intending to be humorous is supported by her equally bantering reply, "Yes, Lord: yet the dogs under the table eat of the children's crumbs" (7:28). In other words, she might be a dog (gentile), but she wasn't asking much—just the crumbs. Jesus responded positively to her humor and plea for help, "For this saying go thy way; the devil is gone out of thy daughter" (7:29).

In similar fashion Jesus' healing of the deaf and stammering man represented a larger issue than simply bringing healing and wholeness to a needy person, as important as that was. Again Jesus was in gentile territory—the region of Decapolis to the east of the Sea of Galilee. Mark's readers would have understood Jesus' action in this gentile stronghold as a call to missionary work. The Good News of the Kingdom of God defies any limitations of race or culture. Christians of every generation are called to faithful proclamation and compassionate service in every place and to all people.

A close look at the story also shows the way Jesus worked. He was always sensitive to the feelings of people, and in this story He wanted to avoid embarrassing the stammering man. Mark tells us that "he took him aside from the multitude" and used a "hands on" method with him. Upon the command "Be opened," the miracle occurred, "... straightway his ears were opened, and the string of his tongue was loosed, and he spake plain."

In these two stirring episodes (7:24–37) we find a striking affirmation of God's power working in Jesus. That power bursts forth in unlikely places and under unusual circumstances. It is experienced by all sorts of people—a quick-witted woman, a deaf-mute man in Decapolis, and sometimes by us.

Some scholars think Mark's account of the feeding of the four thousand (8:1–9) is simply a different version of the earlier story of the feeding of the five thousand (6:35–44). Certainly this story, which is shorter and features different numbers, has striking similarities to the earlier episode.

Short memories.

71

Mark was probably convinced that both events had occurred, however, and the second story makes a slightly different point from the first. In the story about the feeding of the five thousand, the crowd is seen as sheep who need a shepherd. But in this story, Jesus' motive is simple compassion, "I have compassion on the multitude, because they have now been with me three days, and have nothing to eat: And if I send them away fasting to their own houses, they will faint by the way: for divers of them came from afar" (8:2–3).

The similarities between the two stories also underline the continuing lack of understanding by Jesus' disciples. Having been through a comparable experience not long before, why do the disciples bring up the same question again? "From whence can a man satisfy these men with bread here in the wilderness?" (8:4). Will they never learn?

The same lack of understanding afflicted the Pharisees as well. They, too, had witnessed Jesus at work—healing, teaching with authority, and setting people free. Yet they came asking for "a sign from heaven, tempting him" (8:11). Mark comments in his next verse that Jesus "sighed deeply in his spirit." Their spiritual blindness and short memories must have been frustrating and wearisome to Jesus. But He refused to give them any sign other than what had been demonstrated day after day in His ministry. However, by refusing their request, Jesus, once again, incited their opposition in this seventh controversy, over "signs."

Jesus' reply to the Pharisees is instructive to us, too. Often we look for God's activity in the abnormal or spectacular. We ask for indisputable proof that Jesus is the Messiah, the Son of God. The proof may be around us all the time, yet only those with eyes to see and ears to hear are able to identify God's work.

Nine pointed questions.

Indeed, the disciples and the Pharisees seemed to take turns expressing their spiritual thickheadedness. In 8:14–21, Jesus asks nine pointed questions in an effort to help His closest followers understand the meaning of what had been happening. They are in a boat, and the disciples begin to worry because they forgot to bring lunch. In rapid-fire style Jesus' questions erupt: "Why reason ye, because ye have no bread? perceive ye not yet, neither understand? have ye your heart yet hardened? Having eyes, see ye not? and having ears, hear ye not? and do ye not remember? When I brake the five loaves among five thousand, how many baskets full of fragments took ye up?... And when the seven among four thousand, how many baskets full of fragments took ye up?" Jesus' final question is a summary of all the others, "How is it that ye do not understand?" (8:17–21).

It was as if Jesus were saying, "You dodo birds: What more does it take?" And Mark's readers, under pressure and fearful for their lives, would get the point: when we remember who Jesus is, we can face whatever comes.

It is no accident that Mark records the healing of a blind man immediately after the incident in the ship. He addressed the problem of physical blindness just as He had addressed the problem of the disciples' spiritual blindness. The stories are connected, also, by the way they show Jesus' willingness to stand by "blind" persons until they are able to see.

The healing of the blind man at Bethsaida.

The healing of the blind man at Bethsaida (8:22–26) happened gradually in two stages. In the first stage Jesus took the man away from the crowd, touched his eyes with His saliva, and asked him if he were able to see. The man answered, "I see men as trees, walking." Jesus then touched his eyes a second time, and the man was able to see "every man clearly."

In telling this story I believe Mark is trying to help us see that in our early contact with Jesus, as we are just beginning to see who He is, our perception may be hazy. For now, as Paul says, "we see through a glass, darkly; but then face to face." (1 Cor. 13:12).

But as we come to see who Jesus really is and to know His touch, we see life and people with fresh vision. People are no longer perceived as trees walking—as mere objects. It is then that fear gives way to trust, and dramatic signs from heaven are unnecessary. We know who Jesus is, and that is enough.

Lord, help me to be part of Your strategy of approach—to be one of Your followers going out with Your Good News. AMEN.

WHAT THIS SCRIPTURE MEANS TO ME—Mark 6:1–8:26

When I visited the Winchester Cathedral in England, I was fascinated with the large west window. Unlike most cathedral windows, the panels in this one do not contain incidents from the life of Christ or the likenesses of any of the church fathers or of saints. Instead, we see a series of unusual impressionistic designs made by fitting together, in random fashion, pieces of colored and clear glass. This is most unusual for such an ancient ediface.

When I paid my 30 pence so I could take pictures, I began shifting from one spot to another in order to get the best angles from which to shoot this unusual sight. While I hadn't read the descriptive material on the window, I was so absorbed by its panels that I felt compelled to get the best picture I could.

Later that evening I read the cathedral brochure, and I discovered the story of that window and why it is so different.

There was a Civil War in England between the years of 1642 and 1649. The cathedral was severely damaged, and the west window was shattered. The original picture design was gone forever. Some years later, after the monarchy was restored, the fragments from the window, which had been carefully gathered and preserved, were randomly placed in frames along with pieces of clear glass. It is likely that only one or two pieces occupy their original position, but the balance of colored glass with the clear makes a pleasing and striking design. It is undoubtedly the first impressionistic design of its kind, having been completed in 1660.

As I studied that 300-year-old window during my visit, it seemed to speak to me in a special way, but I wasn't quite sure why. After I returned home, though, the reason began to unfold. One night I was showing my travel slides to some friends. When I projected my slide of the west window in the Winchester Cathedral, a young woman, a literary scholar who teaches Comparative Literature at the University of California, asked for a copy. She was intrigued with the design, and it seemed to affect her as it had me.

Some time later I attended a Sunday School class my friend was teaching, and on this particular morning she was using my cathedral window slide to illustrate the lesson. Two Scripture portions were being discussed, Mark 6:33–44 and Mark 8:1–9—two reports of Jesus' miraculous feeding of the crowds who flocked after Him.

In both reports Jesus took the bread that was given to Him, looked up toward heaven, and blessed it. Then He broke it into pieces and gave it to His disciples to distribute among the hungry people. Mark tells us that in both instances there was enough food to go around with quite a bit left over. The loaves and the fish, broken into fragments by Jesus, had satisfied the needs of the crowds.

Suddenly, I saw the parallel between these two miracles of Jesus and my cathedral window and why I had been so moved by it. The original west window panels had been fashioned out of the finest stained glass available in the 13th century. The artists had proudly completed their work, and it was then dedicated in all of its splendor to the glory of God.

Then came that tragic civil war in 1642 in which the cathedral was badly damaged and those magnificent window panels were broken into thousands of fragments. But when the war was over, loving hands gathered up the fragments and fitted them into the new window. The design and shape was vastly different from the original, but since that time, for over 300 years, sunlight has poured through that window and brought joy and blessing to thousands of people. The broken glass fragments and the broken food blessed by Jesus both have served to bring satisfaction to many people, and glory to God.

Now, I realized the full meaning of that west window to me. Now, I understood why I had subconsciously been deeply moved by it. As a young person in high school, I had given my life to God. He then blessed me with a wonderful husband and two beautiful daughters. But after only five and a half years of marriage my husband died. I was broken, but in my grief I gave the fragments of my life back to God. He took the pieces and put together a different picture than I could have imagined. He did what Oswald Chambers said one time, "He made us broken bread and poured out wine to feed others."

In our effort to live for the Lord, all of us, in various ways, experience brokenness—shattered dreams, crippling disappointments, the death of loved ones and friends. But as we let the Lord piece together the fragments, His light can shine through us and into the lives of others. He is the Master Craftsman who is ever ready and anxious to give our lives a new design. This, for me, is the meaning of the miraculously multiplied fragments of the loaves and fish in our Scripture lesson and of the west window of the Winchester Cathedral in England.

LESSON 5
MARK 8:27–10:52

Headed Toward Jerusalem

Illumine my path, Lord, with a knowledge of You and Your Word. AMEN.

Our scene opens in this lesson in Caesarea Philippi. Jesus and His disciples had traveled north from Galilee to this area, which had long been a center of pagan worship. Much of Jesus' public ministry in Galilee is finished at this point, and He will soon head toward Jerusalem. But what takes place here represents a crucial turning point in Mark's Gospel.

The cost of discipleship.

Up to this time Jesus had not openly declared Himself to be the Messiah. Instead, He had tried to "act it out" for His disciples. Now He seems to conclude that they are ready to reflect more deeply on who He is, so He asks the all-important question, "Whom do men say that I am?" (8:27). Their general response identifies Him with John the Baptist or Elijah. Then with penetrating insight and directness Jesus asks, "But whom say ye that I am?" (8:28–29). Up to this point Peter hadn't shown any particular insight, but now he blurts out "Thou art the Christ." Peter's confession identifies Jesus in clear terms—He is not John the Baptist returned to life, nor Elijah, nor some other prophet. He is indeed the long expected Messiah. In response, Jesus acknowledges who He is, but insists they tell no one else (8:30).

Identifying Jesus, however, is only part of the encoun-

ter. Understanding the meaning of His Messiahship is crucial. The popular view of the Messiah was violent and
nationalistic. It held that Israel would see God's power in
action, and her enemies would be broken and defeated.
The Jewish population anticipated a Warrior Prince whose
crusade would liberate their nation.

But now in verse 31 Jesus explains that He as the true
Messiah "must suffer many things," and be rejected by the
Jewish religious leaders, "and be killed, and after three
days rise again." His words carry overtones of Isaiah 53, a
"Suffering Servant" passage, and provide a clue to the
nature of His ministry. This is the first of three predictions
of His coming death and resurrection. Jesus wants all
who profess faith in Him to be aware of the cost of His
Messiahship.

Peter couldn't handle Jesus' incredible words. That the
Messiah should suffer went against the disciples' entire
belief system, and Mark tells in verse 32 that Peter took
Jesus aside and rebuked Him. But Jesus would not be pa-
tronized, and His counterrebuke of Peter reminds us of
His earlier temptation experience in the wilderness, "Get
thee behind me, Satan!" (8:33). Jesus' words sound harsh
and are certainly blunt, because any hint at compromise
had to be repudiated. The stakes were high, and Jesus
wanted no misunderstanding about His mission. Those
who confess Christ must also accept His cross.

We may be more like Peter than we care to admit. We,
too, prefer power without pain; glory without humiliation. Peter was eager to protect Jesus, but Jesus called him,
and us, to follow Him. We are like the little girl who was
asked which famous person in history she would most
like to have been. She replied, "Joan of Arc, but of course, I
wouldn't want to be burned at the stake!"

No one could ever accuse Jesus of inducing others to
follow Him under false pretenses. Jesus didn't offer an
easy way, and He stands in stark contrast to political types
who glibly promise the spoils to the winners. In the short
run, there was no future for the disciples in following
Jesus, but in the long run their confidence could be firmly
fixed in the ultimate will and power of God.

The phrase, "carrying a cross," meant more to Mark's
first-century readers than it does to us. These words have
been emasculated in our vocabulary by misusage, so they
are now a weak metaphor. We often speak of "cross bear-

ing" as an inconvenience or picayune trial, such as a tooth-ache or having to work with a grouchy boss. A nagging spouse, we may say, is "the cross we have to bear."

But that's not what Jesus or Mark meant. Anybody in first-century Palestine was well aware of the cross. There were plenty of examples of slaves and social misfits nailed to crosses along the roadsides. For Jesus to declare that following Him meant taking up a cross (8:34) was a ter-rifying prospect. The Roman occupation of Palestine produced an ongoing run of horror stories. Justice for criminals or any who defied Rome's power was swift, but the agonizing torture of the cross was slow.

"Cross-bearing" and "losing our lives" can have rele-vance for us, however, even though historical circum-stances have radically changed. Christian history is full of examples of persons who went to prison for the sake of conscience. Dietrich Bonhoeffer died in prison at the hands of Nazi cruelty, and his words demonstrate that he fully understood what Jesus meant: "When Jesus calls a man, He bids him come and die." And today there are dedicated and fearless Christians in parts of Africa and eastern bloc nations who are imprisoned psychologi-cally and physically—under constant surveillance and paralyzing restrictions.

Jesus' call is not simply to martyrdom, of course, and He is not promoting asceticism or self-denial for its own sake. The paradox is that we find life in losing it, and we lose our souls by seeking to gain the world. The popular song, "I've Gotta Be Me," is self-centered and narcissistic. Jesus sings of self-fulfillment, too, but His lyrics are made of sterner stuff: "Whoever loses his life for my sake and the gospel's will save it." Those who taste death will still expe-rience the Kingdom of God.

The mountain and the valley.

The Jesus that Mark presents, for all His miracles, per-sonifies humanity. Jesus demonstrated a wide range of emotions—pity, anger, hunger, and weariness. The account of the Transfiguration, however, is different (9:2–13). It occurs just a few days after the Caesarea Phil-ippi experience, on a mountain where Jesus is alone with Peter, James, and John. We don't know for certain what mountain. Tradition gives us two possible sites: Mount Tabor, located in southern Galilee, and Mount Hermon, close by Caesarea Philippi. But we do know that the inner

Mount Hermon as viewed from the Golan Heights with its summertime snowcap. Located approximately twelve miles northeast of Caesarea Philippi, Mount Hermon rises to a height of 9,232 feet above sea level and is considered by some authorities to be the site of the transfiguration of Jesus.

circle, and Mark's readers, are provided here with a glimpse into the future as they experience the Divine Presence: "And his raiment became shining, exceeding white as snow; so as no fuller on earth can white them. And there appeared unto them Elias with Moses: and they were talking with Jesus" (9:3–4).

It was a remarkable experience. Impulsive Peter didn't know what to say, but this hardly kept him from talking. He suggested building three tabernacles to commemorate the event. For the second time in six days Peter was talking when he should have been listening. Mark apologizes for Peter's foot-in-mouthness in 9:6, "For he wist not what to say: for they were sore afraid."

Mark tells us next that a cloud moved in and obscured Jesus and Elijah and Moses, and out of that cloud a voice announced that Jesus was God's "beloved Son" and they should "hear him" (9:7). Then the cloud cleared away, and Moses and Elijah disappeared. Jesus, alone, remained. The meaning of the event is clear. Jesus has not gone to heaven. They were now to leave the mountain and say nothing about what happened until after the resurrection (9:9).

Well, maybe the event wasn't clear to the disciples after

all. Just six days earlier Jesus had referred to His death and resurrection (8:31), and now they were questioning one another as to what "rising from the dead" meant. So they asked Jesus about the long-standing belief that Elijah had to come first before the Messiah would arrive (Mal. 4:5). Jesus' answer to the disciples' question put Him in violent opposition to the teaching of the scribes, and created the eighth controversy recorded by Mark between Jesus and the religious authorities.

In response to their question, Jesus says in so many words, "Correct. He has come, and gone, and now the Son of man is here." Verse 13 is probably a veiled reference to John the Baptist as the new "Elijah" who was the predicted forerunner of Jesus the Messiah.

The scene shifts now as Jesus, Peter, James, and John join the other nine disciples at the foot of the mountain (9:14–29). A large crowd had gathered, and Mark tells us that the scribes were arguing with the disciples. (What else is new?) The nine remaining disciples had failed to heal an epileptic boy. Their failure had made them look bad, and the scribes were pushing their advantage.

Certainly the problem was a tough one. The description of the boy's illness in verse 18 offers classic symptoms of epilepsy, and verse 21 indicates the condition had been life-long. The boy's father was desperate, willing to try any-thing and to seek help from anyone. The disciples had tried to cast out the "dumb spirit" and could not, and so the father turned to Jesus when He came on the scene.

Jesus was perturbed: "O faithless generation, how long shall I be with you? how long shall I suffer you? bring him unto me" (9:19). His frustration was justified. He had just come from a mountaintop experience, and His closest fol-lowers now prove to be impotent healers. It is almost as if Jesus were saying, "Do I have to do it all?"

Perhaps we've gone away on a retreat or had a deeply moving religious experience in which we felt particularly close to God. Upon returning home, however, we find the same old problems and discover the same inability to solve them as before. We need, therefore, to come down to earth quickly as Jesus did. The Transfiguration revealed Jesus to be the Savior of the world, but the immediate problem was the healing of one child. Like the disciples, we can't save the entire world, but we can bring our resources to bear on bite-size events. We can't clean up all of the environment, but we can pick up the trash from the alley in back of our house. The Christian religion provides mountaintop experiences, but it also calls us to work in the valley.

Jesus healed the boy in two stages. In the first stage He rebuked the spirit within the boy and ordered him out. The initial response was not encouraging: "And the spirit cried, and rent him sore, and came out of him...many said, He is dead" (9:26). Then Jesus took the boy by the hand "and lifted him up; and he arose" (9:27). Evidently, things had to get worse before they got better. The incident was a test of the father's faith, and it was a lesson to Jesus' disciples.

The one sliver of hope in the scene that Jesus found when He returned from the mountain was the father's faith, although it was slight. His response to Jesus' challenge, "If thou canst believe, all things are possible to him that believeth" (9:23), was "Lord, I believe; help thou mine unbelief" (9:24). His faith, even though limited, set in motion a series of events that led to his son's cure. He sought help based on the outside bounds of his faith. He trusted as much as he possibly could. Charles Wesley's hymn says it well:

> Faith, mighty faith, the promise sees,
> And looks to that alone;
> Laughs at the impossibilities,
> And cries, it shall be done!

Later, in private, the disciples questioned Jesus as to why they were unable to heal the boy. Jesus' answer is provocative, "This kind can come forth by nothing but by prayer and fasting" (9:29). Prayer is not a pious manipulation of God to get what we want. Instead, it is communing regularly with God so that we gradually increase spiritual power. *Prayerlessness* results in *powerlessness*. The disciples had been unable to help the boy because their spiritual lives weren't nurtured to the degree necessary to do spiritual healing.

Jesus' challenge to the father of the epileptic was not exclusive to first-century Christianity, and the words of Wesley's grand hymn were not exclusive to the eighteenth-century experience. Today we have the faith of a Mother Teresa and a host of unknown Christians who, without fanfare, are living out mountain-moving faith in ministering to the hungry, the starving, the sick, and the dying.

"According to our faith, be it unto us" as we answer God's call to be a friend to the lonely in our neighborhoods and towns...to give and live out a message of hope to those who are discouraged and depressed...to stand alongside the sick and the bereaved.

A hard way to go.

Continuing on their way toward Jerusalem (9:30–50), Jesus and His disciples traveled incognito: "And he would not that any man should know it" (9:30). The implication here is that Jesus wanted to avoid the crowds so He could be alone with His disciples. At this point He needed to instruct and nurture them, which for the moment, took precedent over the concerns and needs of the crowd.

Key to His teaching is the second prediction of the passion, "The Son of man is delivered into the hands of men, and they shall kill him; and after that he is killed, he shall rise the third day" (9:31). This is the briefest of His predictions of the future, but it is also the most sweeping. The words "into the hands of men" is a way of saying Jesus must suffer as a victim of all humankind, not just certain religious rivals or Roman officials. The familiar spiritual, "Were You There When They Crucified My Lord?" could use this verse as its text. Mark is showing that the particular death of Jesus has universal meaning.

A question of greatness.

As usual, the disciples didn't understand, but they were afraid to ask for an explanation (9:32). Instead, they whispered among themselves along the way until Jesus pressed them to share their thoughts aloud. The disciples were reluctant to do so, probably out of embarrassment, because they had been discussing their positions of status within the group: "...for by the way they had disputed among themselves, who should be the greatest" (9:34). Little has changed from those times to now. The tone of their argument has a familiar ring as we remember the daily scramble for position and promotion in a business organization, the jockeying that goes on for appointment or election to a church governing board, and the maneuvering for a prestigious assignment in a social or service club.

But Jesus was patient with them, for next we read that He "sat down" and taught them the meaning of true greatness. "Sitting down" was a way of conveying that a message was important. A rabbi always sat down to teach, and in our slang it would be like saying, "Now listen up, fellows, this is essential." True greatness is a matter of turning the world's priorities upside down.

To get His point across, Jesus employed a visual aid. He took a child on His lap and said that receiving a child was an example of identifying with anyone who needs help. Children in first-century Palestine had no stature, so Jesus was acting out a parable. His embrace of a child was an act of identifying with the lowliest of all.

The next scene, however, indicates that the disciples continued to be slow learners. John reported to Jesus that a man was casting out demons in Jesus' name but was not one of their designated followers (9:38). Jesus' response is a warning against a narrow, sectarian, and exclusive spirit. Healing and helping are not limited to an in-group but are common to all who follow Jesus. The disciples are exposed as being jealous not only of each other, but also of outsiders. Practicing faithfulness without a license is fine with Jesus if the words and deeds authentically represent the God who is revealed in Christ.

There is an important lesson for us in this exchange. The gospel of Jesus Christ is an inclusive fellowship. It loses its power and grandeur if we try to limit it to only our way— our sound and style. Ours is not a time for deifying man-made religious barriers or catering to hyphenated Christians. The words of Jesus have a strong present-day application when He rebuked the disciples for trying to restrain the man who wasn't a member of their group, "Forbid him not; for there is no man which shall do a miracle in my name, that can lightly speak evil of me. For he that is not against us is on our part" (9:39–40).

An inclusive fellowship.

Jesus uses tough talk in 9:42–50 as He elaborates on this point. He minces no words as He pounds home the peril of leading other persons astray. Casting millstones around the necks of people and throwing them into the sea was one form of Roman cruelty. Jesus uses it as an analogy to make His point: causing others to suffer because of your bad example is reason for severe punishment. The demands of discipleship require single-mindedness, and Jesus' figurative language about cutting off hands and feet and plucking out eyes is meant to shake His disciples out of their self-centered complacency.

The picture-language of Mark 9:43 is vivid. The Greek word for "hell" refers to "Gehenna," which was the valley of Hinnom, a ravine south of Jerusalem, which was the city's trash dump. Garbage was burned there, and so the place was synonymous with destruction by fire. Notice that Jesus' strongest language is directed toward two groups: the scribes and Pharisees, the religious leaders of the Jews; and, as here, His own professed disciples. Whenever leaders placed obstacles in the path of ordinary folk who were seeking the Kingdom of God, they earned a tongue-lashing from Jesus.

It was as if Jesus were saying, "Stop this insane squabbling among yourselves. Following me is going to require a commitment that demands sacrifice." And then He called His followers to be like "salt" (verses 49–50). Those disciples whose lives are not characterized by lowly service, openness to others, care for children, and rigorous self-discipline are flavor-less. They have lost the sharpness that sets them apart from the world and makes them useful. The message to His disciples and to us is clear, "Be salty as Christ was salty."

On marriage and divorce. Jesus and His disciples move on. The usual crowd tags along and within it are the familiar faces of Pharisees, people with children, and those wanting something from Him. The Pharisees test Him again as Mark recounts the ninth controversy between Jesus and the Jewish leaders, this time with a problem that was a burning issue among the Jews: the question of divorce (10:2–12). Behind this issue was an argument between two rival rabbinic schools about divorce. The school of Hillel said that a man could get a divorce for the most trivial of reasons—if his wife burned his food, for example. The stricter school of Shammai insisted that unchastity was the only just cause for divorce. Both their interpretations were based on Deuteronomy 24:1–6. In this confrontation with Jesus, the Pharisees were attempting to trap Him into taking one of the sides. It was the old "divide and conquer" ploy they had used before.

In response to their question, "Is it lawful for a man to put away his wife?" (10:2), Jesus asked them to quote the Mosaic law on divorce. When they responded, "Moses suffered to write a bill of divorcement, and to put her away" (10:4), Jesus explained that this provision was made "for the hardness of your heart." And then He went on to argue that lasting marriage was an intention of creation, and in verses 6–8 He quotes from Genesis 1:27.

Rather than focus attention on the loopholes that allow divorce, Jesus shifted the issue to the sacredness of marriage. Jesus declared that although Moses' permission to divorce was a concession to human sin, God intended for a husband and wife to be indissolubly one.

Jesus reminds us of the ideal, of God's intention, but recognizes that in the first century, and in twentieth-century society, as well, people fall far short of the ideal. In Jewish law, women were property. They had no legal rights, but were at the complete disposal of the male head of the family. The Hillel school of thought usually prevailed, and divorce for trivial reasons was common. By His insistence on fidelity in marriage, Jesus bolstered the status of women by restoring a "high" view of the marital vows. Marriage in which "two become one" argues for mutual responsibility, not unilateral action based on personal dissatisfaction.

This part of our Scripture lesson is a hard one to apply to the complex problems of divorce in the modern world. Some say that Jesus simply and unequivocally prohibited divorce. Others argue that Jesus was not a legalist, and what we have here is the reminder that God wills marriage to be an indissoluble union. It represents the norm, but apparently divorce is sometimes necessary because of human failure. Even then, there is the sense that God's intention is being violated. As one divorced woman put it, "Divorce is not the sin. The selfishness and hostility that lead to a divorce are the sins." Jesus calls us to take the high view of marriage, but His own willingness to forgive sinners makes room in the Kingdom for those who fall short. And all of us can be grateful for that.

Children and the Kingdom.

Jesus was on His way to the cross. He knew it, and He had explained it to His disciples on two occasions, even though His words didn't sink into their understanding. Yet, in this next scene we see Him taking time for children who, as we've seen, were persons without status in that society (10:13–16).

According to custom, mothers often brought their children after their first birthday to be touched and blessed by a rabbi. This may have accounted for the scene here, and probably the children were infants. The disciples, however, maintained their unblemished record for inappropri-

85

ate behavior by rebuking the parents who had brought their children to Jesus. To be fair to the disciples, Mark's verb tense suggests that these parents were becoming a nuisance, for one reading of 10:13 is "they kept on bringing their small children" to Jesus. Any pastor attempting to preach to a congregation full of anxious mothers holding squirming, crying babies can identify with the disciples. To them, teaching, preaching, and doing miracles of healing were surely more important than fooling around with squalling kids.

But Jesus does both. He teaches and He embraces the children at the same time. His point seems to be that the Kingdom belongs to the childlike. What makes children so apt an illustration is not their innocence but their simplicity and ability to trust. Children are helpless and dependent. One way of interpreting verse 15 is "The Kingdom belongs to such as these, the children; and if you do not receive God's gift as a child receives gifts from earthly parents, you shall not enter."

The rich young ruler and the Kingdom.

The contrast between Jesus' words about childlikeness and His encounter with the rich young man (10:17–22) is striking. The broken and the needy—if they know it—are far closer to the Kingdom of God than those who are adequate and successful. Mark's placing the story of Jesus and the children back to back with that of the rich young man was probably no accident.

Not that the young man was so bad. In fact, he had much to commend him. But he got off on the wrong foot with Jesus by attempting to "snow" him with an ingratiating phrase, "Good Master, what shall I do that I may inherit eternal life?" (10:17). Jesus responded by saying, in effect, "Don't use flattery by calling me good. Save that for God." Then He recites several commandments, as a kind of checklist: don't commit adultery, do not kill, do not steal, do not bear false witness, defraud not, honor thy father and mother (10:19).

The rich young man is confident he has passed the test, "Master, all these have I observed from my youth." It is interesting that Jesus didn't dispute the young man's reply, but then He presented him with the acid test: dispose of your wealth and follow me. In fact, verse 21 contains a five-fold imperative that curled the young man's toes inside his sandals: go, sell, give, come, follow. For this particular young man, getting rid of his wealth was a pre-requisite to discipleship. But he failed the test. It was too much for him, and he responded by becoming the only man in Mark's Gospel who was called by Jesus but who chose not to follow.

Jesus next moved from the specifics of His encounter with the rich young man to a generalization about the problems wealth brings (10:23–27). His view of riches as a hindrance is another popular Jewish belief that Jesus turned upside down. Traditionally, wealth was a sign of blessing by God. Here, Jesus presented it as a major obsta-cle to a right relationship with God. The following para-phrase of verses 23–27 captures the essence of Jesus' attitude, "How hard, indeed, is it for *anyone* to enter the Kingdom, but for rich people it is quite impossible. In fact, humanly speaking, it is impossible for anyone to be saved, rich or not; but with God all things are possible."

The problems of wealth.

The disciples were "astonished" (10:24) at Jesus' words, but He then compounded their shock by using an analogy to illustrate what He meant by "impossible." He says that a camel could go through the eye of a needle more easily than a rich man could enter the Kingdom. Jesus was prob-ably exaggerating, maybe even joking, by using this phrase. But like most humor, there was important truth about human nature hidden within it. What we own often ends up owning us, but material possessions are very low priorities in the Kingdom of God.

Good old Peter, setting modesty aside, congratulates himself and his fellow disciples by saying to Jesus, "We have left all, and have followed thee" (10:28). His implica-tion is clear: "What about us?" In response, Jesus declared that there were compensations for discipleship, both in this world and the next, which far outweigh the suffering and persecution that are part of the discipleship experi-ence (10:29–31).

Mark's earliest readers might have understood Jesus' words better than the disciples did. Those persecuted early Christians became members of an intimate and warm fel-lowship. They experienced a depth of caring for one an-other far richer than their natural families provided. The reward for becoming Christian was not simply other-worldly. Mark reminded his readers that they had experi-enced a fellowship and loyalty so deep, it was payment worth "a hundredfold" for what they had sacrificed. In the Kingdom a new family is given, and in the final accounting "many that are first shall be last; and the last first" (10:31).

Spiritual and physical blindness.

The vivid picture of Jesus striding ahead of His disciples as He walked toward His fate must have been an unforgettable experience for those who were following Him (10:32–50). The emotions of the group intensified as they approached Jerusalem. Mark tells that the disciples were both "amazed" and "afraid" (10:32). With great patience, Jesus paused to explain one more time what was going to happen to Him. This was the third, final, and most detailed prediction of His coming suffering and death. Two new dimensions were introduced: His transfer to a Roman court, and, the ridicule, contempt, and beating He would experience.

Given this clear description of the indignities to come, the response of James and John was a monument to insensitivity (10:35–37). In spite of what Jesus had just told them, they still expected an extravaganza when they reached Jerusalem, and they wanted ringside seats—favored positions in the Kingdom of God. Did they hear only what they wanted to hear? Do we?

In responding, Jesus teaches them and us two important lessons (10:38). One is that, whatever rewards come from following Jesus, they belong only to those who share the journey. In so many words Jesus asks, "Can you go through the terror that I will have to go through?"

The other lesson is about servanthood. The goal of the Christian is not to be chief, but to be servant. The life of Jesus had been a model of serving, not being served. His death was like a ransom, and it provided a final capstone to what His life had demonstrated. Jesus' life had been lived for others, and His death was for the sake of others. Both are models *par excellence* for us to follow.

By the time they reached Jericho, they were only fifteen miles from Jerusalem. Out of the crowd blind Bartimaeus called out, "Jesus, thou son of David, have mercy upon me!" (10:46). People tried to quiet him, but Bartimaeus would have none of it, and he kept crying out to Jesus, "Thou son of David, have mercy on me." Jesus heard him, and Bartimaeus came forward when Jesus singled him out, "What wilt thou that I should do unto thee?" In response Bartimaeus said, "Lord, that I might receive my sight." And in verse 52 Jesus said, "Go thy way; thy faith hath made thee whole." Jesus restored his sight, performing the last recorded healing miracle in Mark's Gospel.

Verse 52 tells us that healed Bartimaeus "followed Jesus in the way." His spiritual vision matched his restored physical sight. The Greek word for "receive my sight" (10:51) is *anableps*. Ironically, the same Greek word is used to identify a species of fish that has two sets of eyes, one pair for underwater vision and a second pair for seeing on the surface. Bartimaeus, also, saw in two new ways. His physical vision was the gift Jesus gave him, but he also acquired new spiritual eyes, which enabled him to know who his healer was.

Blind Bartimaeus discovered that believing is seeing. Jesus' disciples saw with blurred vision, and so do we. Mark's Gospel helps us see Jesus more clearly in the hope that we also might believe. And follow.

Let the truths I've learned in this lesson guide me today, Lord. AMEN.

WHAT THIS SCRIPTURE MEANS TO ME
—Mark 8:27–10:32

Growing up in the southwestern part of the United States gave me a perspective of Israel and some aspects of life that Jesus might have encountered long before I learned about the geography of the land where He lived. In southern Arizona, dusty roads, dusty tables, and dusty air were a part of our lives.

We had only one car, which my Dad drove to work. Anywhere the rest of us needed to go when Dad was at work was either by city bus or, as Mother put it, by "shank's mare"—walking! Not all of the streets in our part of town were paved. So we got pretty dusty, just walking to the store four blocks away.

We were never idle, either. If there were spare minutes, we had things to keep our hands busy. Mother's philosophy handed down from her grandmother, to her mother, and then on to my sister and me, was "idle hands are the devil's workshop." We couldn't have *that* in our house!

As a child, I made toys out of oatmeal boxes, wood blocks sawed from the ends of 2 × 4's, Log Cabin syrup cans (those wonderful house-shaped tin cans that we threw away by the score. Oh, how I wish I had a few of those today!), or even a box. If it were small and empty, I gave it an identity and filled it with imagination. It kept my sister and me out of trouble and out of mother's hair. During World War II, the trees in the yard became airplanes and we were pilots, bombardiers, navigators, or soldiers. In our imaginations we fought many of the battles of the war in our yards and in those trees.

For me, these childhood memories make our lesson come alive. Mark helps us see that Jesus was always imaginatively busy—so busy, in fact, that He seldom had time to be alone or to rest. The roads He walked were dusty, and the climate was hot. But none of this stopped Him as He ministered to and cared for the people He met.

To Jesus, ministry was synonymous with servanthood. Ministry meant caring for people. As He lived with His disciples twenty-four hours a day, He was trying to help them understand that they were to concentrate on "the things that be of God" and not on "the things that be of men" (8:33). And Jesus' interests in helping others were the same as God's.

So often, in our efforts to serve the Lord, our priorities seem to get out of order. We strive for prominence, for seats in the front row, for leadership roles. But this is not the servant model Jesus gave us. We don't see Him heading committees or "directing traffic." Instead, our picture of Jesus in the Gospel of Mark is one of action. He is walking dusty and hot roads. He is caring for children and healing the sick and miserable. In other words, He is busy meeting the needs of people—not like Martha who was busy about "many things," but careless at times about personal relationships. Our role, like that of Jesus, is to concentrate on the things of God and be sensitive, even when we're busy, to the needs of others.

At times our roads in life may be dusty, like the Arizona streets and roads of my childhood. Or the air of our lives may be smoggy as it is in so many of our cities today, or the people we're trying to help may seem unappreciative and critical of our feeble efforts. But in spite of all this, Jesus has called us to be His servants in our imperfect world—servants not preoccupied with "the things that be of men," but busy in fulfilling our mission of helping and serving others for the Lord.

LESSON 6
MARK 11:1—12:44

The Ministry in Jerusalem

Lord, help me to "study, to show myself approved." AMEN.

Jesus' triumphal entry into Jerusalem was an act of symbolism that He had deliberately planned. His actions give every indication of being a fulfillment of Zechariah's prophetic words, "Rejoice greatly, O Daughter of Zion; shout, O Daughter of Jerusalem: behold, thy King cometh unto thee: he is just, and having salvation; lowly, and riding upon an ass, and upon a colt the foal of an ass" (Zech. 9:9).

In the opening words of our Scripture lesson we read how methodically Jesus planned this event. First, He instructed two of His disciples to go to a certain place in the village where they would find a colt that had never been ridden before. Second, He told them exactly what to say to the colt's owner in order to secure permission to use the animal, "The Lord hath need of him."

Next, Mark tells us that the two disciples followed Jesus' instructions, and everything turned out exactly as He said it would (11:1–6). Jesus then mounted the colt, and His procession moved down the road the short distance to Jerusalem. While the crowd along the way responded enthusiastically to Jesus, it isn't certain at all that they understood the full meaning of what was happening. The quotation in Mark 11:9, "Hosanna; Blessed is he that cometh in the name of the Lord," comes from Psalm 118:26. In

Jesus' triumphal entry into Jerusalem.

The Old City of Jerusalem as viewed from the Mount of Olives. It was down these slopes and up through the Valley of Kidron that Jesus went when He made His Triumphal Entry into Jerusalem.

those days that phrase was used as a greeting for all pilgrims on their way to a religious festival. It is true that the words in verse 10 refer explicitly to the Kingdom of David. They make a statement of hope for the Messiah, which points to the idea that this One would be a political and military leader.

It is likely that Jesus chose this way of entering Jerusalem because He knew that those who understood Him and His mission would recognize the meaning of the symbolism. Those who didn't would simply shout "Hosanna" as a spontaneous response to a parade.

For Mark's readers, looking back from their side of the cross, the scene was loaded with meaning. They would have remembered that the crisis that led to Jesus' crucifixion began with His triumphal entry, and they would have recalled how the disciples followed along in their own bewildered way. They would also remember that lurking behind the cries of exaltation were the religious authorities who were waiting to strike at just the right moment. And in the midst of it all was Jesus, a solitary and sorrowful figure, determined to press on to the concluding events of His ministry.

A view of the Kidron Valley from the south.

Before going on, let's go back for a moment and look again at some of the rather interesting details associated with the early stages of this event. Note that the colt was tied up at a prearranged location. Then, too, there was apparently a predetermined "password" between the colt's owner—"Why do ye this?" and Jesus—"The Lord has need of him." The event suggests that Jesus already had active followers in Jerusalem. Over and over again in Mark's Gospel, as we've seen, the ministry and message of Jesus have been partially secret and usually unadvertised. But now Jesus emerges from relative obscurity into the public eye. Jesus and His followers could have entered Jerusalem simply and quietly, but now He chose to arrive in a dramatic fashion.

However, even though His movements were public and ceremonious, Jesus' actions delivered a different message than was popularly expected. He entered as a "lowly hero," a phrase that seems to contradict itself. His followers were a motley crew, but He was more of a king than the crowds realized.

During this scene Jesus doesn't say anything. But we listen to the cry of the crowd, "Hosanna!" which means

"Save, now" or "Save, I pray." Jesus' silence as He rides along astride a donkey suggests an unspoken reply, "I am the Messiah, and I will save; but not in the way you expect."

The significance of this scene for you and me parallels its meaning for early Christians. Jesus calls His followers to be "Lowly heroes and heroines." The religious film, *The Parable,* captured this idea quite well. In that movie Jesus is portrayed as a clown, the subject of ridicule, and a ludicrous figure, much like a king riding on a donkey. He is both followed and hated by the crowd. He does not portray the Messiah that people expect, yet He comes to serve them and God.

Mark's Gospel has slowly and surely revealed who Jesus is. The recording of the triumphal entry of Jesus into Jerusalem fits an established pattern. Jesus' act was an announcement, but it wasn't explicit. The people shouted the proper words, but it seems clear that they didn't understand the full implications of what they were saying. While Jesus intentionally "went public" at this time, it wasn't clear even to His disciples who He really was, until after the cross and the resurrection.

Jesus' impatience with hypocrisy.

What happened next in Mark's account is hard to understand without background information. Jesus is returning from Bethany where He and His disciples had spent the night. He is hungry. He sees a fig tree, but it has no figs on it "for the time of the figs was not yet" (11:13). Jesus then behaves in what appears to be a most uncharacteristic manner: He condemns the tree. "No man shall eat fruit of thee hereafter forever. And his disciples heard it" (11:14). The story is completed later in 11:20,21, when they find "the fig tree dried up from the roots."

Because this action is so uncharacteristic of Jesus, most commentators believe this was an enacted parable. It was, in other words, an act that made a statement. The earliest commentator on Mark's Gospel, Victor of Antioch in the fifth century, said that Jesus "used the fig tree to set forth the judgment that was about to fall on Jerusalem." (He was referring to the terrible devastation of Jerusalem in A.D. 70.) Israel, particularly its leaders, had produced leaves that could be observed but there was no fruit. Jesus was denouncing sterile religion and leaders who fail to provide spiritual direction and power.

Another reason for concluding that the fig tree story

was an enacted parable is its location in Mark. Like bread in a sandwich, the verses that tell the story surround another event that illustrates the point of the parable. The story in the middle describes the overthrow of the money changers in the temple (11:15–19). Self-centered religious leaders are like fruitless fig trees.

In this middle story we see Jesus entering the temple, undoubtedly the forecourt—the place where non-Jews were allowed to pray. This outer court, known as the Court of the Gentiles, was a place where people of other races could meet God. Sadly, it had become a place where all kinds of peripheral activities were occurring, chief of which was the selling of sacrificial animals. Religious hucksters peddled "purified" doves for sacrifices. The doves used in the temple sacrifice had to be without blemish, and temple inspectors invariably found birds purchased outside to be "impure." The unblemished doves available in the forecourt were sold at an inflated price, and religious pilgrims who came to worship were regularly exploited. In addition to the dove-hucksters there were money changers who exchanged Roman money for Jewish coins. Only Jewish money could be used to pay temple dues, so the money changers provided a service, which had come to be a rip-off because of the high rate of exchange—an enormous profit for the priests.

A middle story.

Jesus' response was full-force anger. When He first arrived in Jerusalem, He had visited the temple and "looked round about upon all things" (11:11). It may be that He had sized up the situation at that time and took action immediately upon His return later.

In these verses Jesus sounds and behaves like an Old Testament prophet, quoting Isaiah 56:7 and Jeremiah 7:11. He reminds the temple scribes and priests that the forecourt was to be "of all nations the house of prayer," but "ye have made it a den of thieves" (11:17).

The anger of Jesus' words was matched by His actions, as He threw out the money changers and the hucksters and wrecked the place. He also put a stop to the common practice of using the outer court as a shortcut for traffic: "And (he) would not suffer that any man should carry any vessel through the temple" (11:16). Jesus demonstrated fierce impatience with all prostitutions of faith, and this encounter is the most dramatic example. Certainly the

Jerusalem as viewed from the slopes of the Mount of Olives. The Dome of the Rock, built in the seventh century and located in the center of the picture, is the site of the temple of Jesus' day.

scribes and chief priests got the message, and they intensified their efforts to destroy Jesus (11:18).

The parallel between this story and our churches today is striking. Peripheral activities, money-raising events, gambling, when done in the name of Christ, can undermine the spiritual intentions of Christianity. Jesus attacked the money changers and the peddlers because they had confused the world and the temple. They had become lump instead of leaven. And that is our danger, too.

On faith and prayer. Next, we see that Jesus changed the subject when the disciples focused on the incident of the fig tree. This is another reason to believe that the fig tree episode was an enacted parable. In Mark 11:22–26 Jesus teaches the disciples a lesson about faith and prayer by using a startling figure of speech.

"Removing a mountain" was a common expression for describing a situation that was virtually impossible. In those times, teachers were sometimes called "mountain-removers" because of their efforts to remove mountains of ignorance and confusion.

Jesus is telling them here that prayer without faith doesn't stand a chance. And Mark seems to place Jesus' teaching here on faith and prayer immediately after two dramatic condemnations of spiritual sterility, so that the disciples will see and understand the only antidote for religious impotence.

Three conditions are essential if prayer is to "move mountains." "Faith," stated here both negatively ("and shall not doubt in his heart") and positively ("but shall believe that those things which he saith shall come to pass") is a prerequisite (11:23). "Expectation" is also vital: "What things soever ye desire, when ye pray, believe that ye receive them, and ye shall have them" (11:24). And "forgiveness" (11:26) is necessary because lingering bitterness or leftover feelings of resentment nullify our prayers.

We need only to evaluate our prayers by these standards to see the source of our own spiritual impotence. Probably the early church remembered these sayings of Jesus as clearly as any simply because they were basic to life in the Christian community. The church is a community of faith and prayer, or it is an empty shell. Christians are persons who pray with faith and expectation, with a forgiving spirit, or they are impotent.

The day after the events we have just studied occurred, Jesus returned to Jerusalem and was walking in the temple. There He was confronted by the chief priests, scribes, and elders. It is quite likely He was walking in what was called the Royal Cloister of the temple's outer court where rabbis taught and debated ideas. We can assume that their question, "By what authority doest thou these things?" (11:28) referred to what had happened the day before when Jesus had cleared the temple. At one level they were asking, "Who do you think you are to come storming in here upsetting (literally!) our operation? Who named *you* chief reformer?"

A question of authority.

Their question was menacing. They were not really seeking information. They were just trying to put Him in a corner. Jesus, however, stayed within the rules of good debate technique, and instead of answering them directly, He posed a counterquestion, "The baptism of John, was it from heaven, or men? Answer me" (11:30).

Jesus' reply was shrewd. He was obviously a lot sharper than His opponents. They thought they had trapped Him by their question about His authority. If He had said His authority came from God, they could have accused Him of blasphemy. On the other hand if He had said it came from secular authorities, His cleansing of the temple would have been an act of insurrection. His counterquestion, however, put them immediately on the defense.

If they replied that John's baptism was not approved by God, the people who loved and admired John would be offended and outraged. If they said it was from God, then Jesus, who was identified with John, could say that His authority also had divine blessing. Jesus' question forced His adversaries to remember John's call to repentance, his message of forgiveness, and, most important, his announcement, "There cometh one mightier than I after me…" (1:7).

Their only possible response was the first-century version of the Fifth Amendment, "We cannot tell" (11:33). They could not have answered because they would have incriminated themselves. For this reason, Jesus was not obligated to answer their question. We learn from this that Jesus does not commit Himself to any who do not commit themselves to truth. And Jesus' message to us is equally sobering. If we ask, "Who are you, Jesus?" He is likely to turn our question around and ask, "Who do you believe I am?"

In taking us behind the scene of this revealing confrontation of Jesus with the Jewish authorities, Mark illuminates the intense controversy that raged over Jesus' authority. The outrage was escalating, and ultimately led to His arrest, trial, and crucifixion.

The parable of the vineyard.

Jesus' dialogue with the scribes, chief priests, and elders continued (12:1–12). He told them a parable that also had to do with authority—theirs and how they had abused it! Jesus' parables are not usually allegories. They are stories that stand on their own and do not have symbolic meanings. But the parable of the vineyard is an exception; it is a cross between an allegory and a parable.

The vineyard stands for Israel, and its owner represents God. The tenants in the story are the Jewish religious leaders; the servants include the Old Testament prophets and possibly John the Baptist. The owner's son, of course, represents Jesus.

The story moves through four stages. First (12:1–5), the tenants (Jewish religious leaders) rebel against the owner (God) by rejecting, beating, and killing a succession of servants (prophets). Second (12:6), the owner goes far beyond normal expectations and sends his son (Jesus) in one final effort to receive the fruit of the vineyard that is owed to him. Third (12:7–8), the servants kill the son, demonstrating the self-serving abuse of the authority entrusted to them. And fourth (12:9), the owner rejects the faithless stewardship of the tenants and decides to entrust the vineyard to others.

Next, Jesus changes His metaphor (12:10–11) to emphasize a final point: the church with Christ as the cornerstone is God's new hope. Israel had violated a sacred trust, and the parable-allegory predicts the end of one chapter in history and the beginning of another. To illustrate His point, Jesus quotes a selection from their own Scriptures, Psalm 118:22–23, to describe their condemnation. It is bitter irony.

Jesus' enemies understood perfectly what He was saying. The allegory was absolutely clear to them. They were condemned by their arrogance. Jesus had challenged them: accept my words or kill me. And they would have killed Him on the spot, but they were afraid such action at that time would incite a riot.

A question of God and country.

The first wave of attack by the religious leaders had been repulsed, "They left him and went their way" (12:12). Fresh troops were sent to challenge Jesus. This time, we read certain Pharisees and Herodians came "to catch him in his words" (12:13). Their question was couched in flattery as insincere as their souls, "Master, we know that thou art true, and carest for no man: for thou regardest not the person of men, but teachest the way of God in truth" (12:14). Their statement oozes hypocrisy.

Mark introduces us here to the eleventh controversy in his Gospel: civil obedience—God versus country. This was an issue in Jesus' day, even as it is in ours. Politics and religion are always touchy subjects.

Jesus' inquisitors were clever, and they stated the question in classic form, "Is it lawful to give tribute to Caesar, or not?" (12:14). They had chosen a burning dilemma for this entrapment, one that had divided the Jews since a head tax or "census" was imposed by the Romans in A.D. 6. The extreme nationalists, or Zealots, had refused to pay it and instigated a brief and unsuccessful revolt against Rome. The tax continued to be unpopular, and resistance to it was a touchy subject with the government.

The issue, as they put it, called for a decision as to whether one ought to obey a law imposed by a government of occupation. If Jesus said "yes," He would have offended the people who shared the sentiments (if not the practice) of the Zealots. If He said "no," He could be denounced to the Roman authorities as an insurrectionist.

Their mistake was their oversimplification. Jesus did not accept the "either/or-ness" of their hypocritical query. There is no question but that we owe some things to the state, however, we owe something radically different to God. The fact that the Pharisees and the Herodians had a coin when Jesus asked them for one, actually incriminated them. They admitted to having Caesar's currency, so they were committed to paying taxes in that coin. He seems to be saying, "Caesar's image is on the coin. It is his money. You've already involved yourselves in his value system. But don't forget: God has a different kind of claim on our lives" (12:17).

Jesus turned a trick question into an occasion for teaching a basic principle for ethical decisions. He does not tell us what to do, but He offers guidelines about how to make a decision. His point seems to be, though, that since we receive certain benefits from the state, we ought to pay for them with the money that has "Caesar's imprint" on it. But we also have the imprint of God on us; we are created in His image. Our primary obligation in life is to Him.

A serious answer to a silly question.

The next group to challenge Jesus was the Sadducees (12:18–27). They were very conservative priestly aristocrats who refused to accept any Scriptures as valid other than the five books of Moses—Genesis through Deuteronomy—and they rejected any later theological innovations including the resurrection of the body. The haughty and arrogant Sadducees were unpopular with the people because they openly collaborated with the Romans. This is the only time in the Gospel of Mark that the Sadducees appear on the scene. But to them goes the dubious honor of instigating another bitter controversy between Jesus and the religious authorities—this time on the subject of the resurrection.

They present Jesus with a hypothetical situation, which, in their minds, will demonstrate the absurdity of believing in an afterlife (12:19–23). The situation they pose is based on instructions given in Deuteronomy 25:5, "If brethren dwell together, and one of them die, and have no child, the wife of the dead shall not marry without unto a stranger: her husband's brother shall go in unto her, and take her to him to wife, and perform the duty of an husband's brother unto her." This provision of the Mosaic Law, known as Levirate marriage, was instituted so that family names and property could be carried on. The Sadducees twist this concept now to fit a ridiculous situation in which seven brothers die without children, each having in turn taken the childless wife of the older brother. Then, in an attempt to stump Jesus and spoof the idea of resurrection, they ask whose wife she would be in the afterlife.

Jesus responds to their ludicrous question with a double accusation. First, He accuses them of not knowing their own Scriptures. Second, He indicts them for failing to trust the power of the living God (12:24). In making this second point Jesus refers to Exodus 3:6, which makes it clear that the God of the Patriarchs is the God of the living, not the dead. In speaking to Moses from the burning bush God said, "I am the God of thy father, the God of Abraham, the God of Isaac, and the God of Jacob." The present tense form used here indicates that the patriarchs are alive with God. Then Jesus goes on to challenge the Sadducees to think in fresh categories. They viewed resurrection in terms of the temporal forms of this life, whereas afterlife occurs in eternal circumstances. The resurrected are "as the angels which are in heaven" (12:25).

The Sadducees knew the Scripture a little bit, but they did not know the Spirit that interpreted it. They were trapped by their own wooden literalism. Unfortunately, they have many counterparts today. Those who misuse and twist Scripture to support their own ideas, instead of listening to the Bible to hear what God is saying, are today's Sadducees. In effect, Jesus confronted them with a blunt statement, "You are wrong in the question you ask." They were guilty of the ancient yet very modern game of trivial pursuit—how many angels can sit on the head of a pin.

The lesson for us in our day is to avoid playing dangerous games with our Scriptures. Rather, we are to listen prayerfully and openly to what the God of the living has to say to us in His Word.

The first commandment.

Unlike the scoffing, contemptuous Sadducees, the scribe who next appears before Jesus gives every indication of being sincere and honest in his search for answers (12:28–34). When we know that the rabbis identified 613 different commandments in the law, the question, "which is first?" seems reasonable.

Jesus responds by citing two Old Testament passages, Deuteronomy 6:4 and Leviticus 19:18. However, He puts them together in a way that had not been done before. Verses 29–30 are from the *Shema,* a prayer which devout Jews repeated daily. Reciting basic beliefs about God ("Hear, O Israel, the Lord our God is one Lord") was a way of reminding pious Jews of God's total claim on their lives. The Shema was probably the answer the scribe expected, but Jesus changed its meaning by adding the Leviticus passage, "...thou shalt love thy neighbor as thyself." The point Jesus was making is that while the love of God is of transcendent importance; if it is not associated with obligations to one's neighbor, it is inevitably self-centered. In its original context, loving thy "neighbor" had to do with a Jew's treatment of other Jews. But Jesus here speaks of it without boundaries. The old law was invested with new meaning.

The scribe understood the point Jesus was making and responded positively (12:32). He seemed to understand that loving God and loving others exposed the elaborate sacrificial system of Judaism as a spiritually barren ritual. And Jesus' response to the scribe is encouraging, "Thou art not far from the Kingdom of God" (12:34).

While the scribe was "not far from the Kingdom," Jesus' sworn enemies in the surrounding crowd were not happy. For them, this represented a major controversy over the interpretation of the Law. And while they were forced to be silent for the moment, their evil intentions would soon erupt into violence.

In Mark 12:35 we get an answer from Jesus without knowing the question, "How say the scribes that Christ is the Son of David?" Whatever He was asked, His reply addresses His own relationship to a long-standing belief that the Messiah would be a Son of David. The popular image of a "Son of David" for the "Messiah" was misleading and inadequate. It was simply a concern about genealogy and therefore a trivial matter. Jesus was, in fact, a descendant of David, but that was not the most important point. He was trying, once again, to deny the idea that the Messiah was to be a nationalistic warrior who was coming to establish an earthly empire. Jesus was saying, "The true messiah is David's *Lord,* not simply his descendant." In saying that, He created another controversy over the true meaning of the Messiah's descent from King David.

Redefining prominence.

In response to all of this discussion Mark tells us that the "common people heard him gladly." We can be sure the scribes, however, did not hear gladly what Jesus said next in verses 38–40. Here we read that Jesus in rapid succession accuses the scribes of being status-seeking, privilege-demanding stuffed shirts who take advantage of widows! They were full of pride, dressing to attract attention and occupying the front rows in the synagogue.

We are well advised to pay close attention to Jesus' strong words. The specific reference in Mark 12:40 was probably to the scribal practice of accepting fees for performing religious services to widows. But now as then, persons who experience grief are vulnerable to those who will exploit them in the name of religion. Unsolicited opportunities to "capture memories of the deceased" often come to mourners shortly after the funeral. They may take the form of a laminated newspaper notice of the loved one's death, or the opportunity to make a contribution as a memorial gift to one cause or another. Then as now, exploiting widows—or anyone for that matter—in the name of religion is contemptible.

Jesus' warning to the scribes has a practical application for us today. We are not to use our Christian position for personal gain as the scribes did. This condemnation of their pretentious showmanship and greed was indeed a bitter pill for them to swallow. It kindled a controversy that could not be ignored because it went so solidly against the grain of all they held dear.

A vivid example of commitment and sacrifice.

Immediately the scene shifts and Jesus gives us a vivid contrast between people in "high places" behaving in low ways and the widow who dropped her two mites into the treasury (12:41–44). The farthing that the woman gave was the smallest unit of money in the currency at that time, but it was all she had. It is certain that as Jesus stood by watching that day that He saw many people give larger amounts of money. But when this widow dropped in her two little coins, He commended her for giving more. Hers was a sacrificial gift; it was all she had!

In this moving story that closes our lesson, a vivid example of commitment and sacrifice stands in stark contrast to the previous one of self-interest, exploitation, and greed. This was an important word for Mark's earliest readers. They were a minority facing death and despair. They were hounded by both civil and religious authorities to give all they had. But unlike the scribes and the Pharisees, Jesus approved of them. And they came to understand, like the Mother Teresa's of the late twentieth century, that it is by giving that we receive.

Help me, Lord, to not be too preoccupied with Your return, but to "take heed, watch, and pray," until You come. AMEN.

WHAT THIS SCRIPTURE MEANS TO ME
—Mark 11:1–13:37

The crisp, aroma-filled mountain air swelled our smog-tainted lungs and rejuvenated our city-weary bodies. We were at a remote campsite high in the San Bernardino Mountains of southern California, almost a hundred miles east of Los Angeles. It was a girls' camp, and on this particular morning I had my cabin group clustered around me for devotions.

Suddenly the silence was broken by a loud C-R-A-C-K! It sounded like a high-powered rifle shot, and then everything was quiet again. It was difficult not to stop what we were doing and check out the noise, but we resisted the temptation and continued our meditation on the life of David.

Later, while the girls were busy with their other morning activities, I went to investigate. After walking through the forest that surrounded the campgrounds, I finally came upon a giant fir tree that had fallen right across the main road leading into the camp. It was a beautiful tree with a sturdy looking trunk, finely checked bark, and shiny green leaves. I wondered: What had caused this magnificent giant to fall?

As I walked around the tree, my curiosity was aroused. Then I came to where it had split off the lower trunk, and I saw that it was hollow inside. When I stooped over for a closer look, I saw what looked like millions of ants swarming all over the inside of the decayed trunk. Those tiny, crawling things had literally eaten out the heart of that giant tree until there was nothing left inwardly to support it.

I stood back and reflected on that strange sight. Suddenly, it struck me that in the quiet and secluded setting of this mountain forest, my heavenly Father had just given me a vivid object lesson. I was reminded of the Lord's words of warning which are threaded through our Scripture lesson. Here, Mark described a number of encounters Jesus had with the Jewish religious leaders, the scribes, Pharisees, and Sadducees. They had repeatedly challenged, questioned, and baited Him.

These rigid legalists were living superficial lives. On the outside they looked pious and religious. They followed all of the man-made rules of behavior, but on the inside the hearts of these religious leaders were eaten out by pride and ego and a superficial following of the Law. They looked holy, but on the inside they were the fulfillment of Ezekiel's descriptive words, "I saw every form of creeping things, and abominable beasts and all the idols of the house of Israel" (Ezek. 8:10).

Their superficial and hollow piety grieved the heart of Jesus then, even as it does now. It is tragically easy for us to become so involved with the letter of the law that we lose its spirit. And when this happens, we become judgmental of any who don't see things just the way we do. If their vocabulary or patterns of worship differ from ours, we tend to write them off. We allow feelings of bitterness to take root in our lives—we become self-centered in our interpretation of the good news of the gospel until it becomes exclusive instead of inclusive. We give a little here and fudge a little there until we become hollowed out and decayed on the inside. And for a time our act may hold together, but through it all the Lord knows what's on the inside, and in time others will see beyond our masks, too.

But as we daily turn our hearts over to the Lord and as our roots become deeply imbedded in the love of God, there need be no fear or concern over the possibility of inner hollowness or decay. The promise Jesus gave His disciples long ago, "Lo, I am with you always," holds good for us today. Even in the midst of our struggles and humanness, as we grow in trust and faith, the same Jesus who so tenderly instructed and guided His disciples will help us to stand tall in our spiritual life and practice.

LESSON 7
MARK 13:1–14:72

The Beginning of the End

Lord, let what I study become part of my daily life. AMEN.

Mark's thirteenth chapter is an extremely difficult part of Scripture for us twentieth-century Christians to understand. Its imagery is vividly Jewish in form and draws heavily on the words of such Old Testament prophets as Daniel, Amos, Isaiah, and Joel.

Sometimes referred to as "the little apocalypse," this chapter offers a particular way of thinking about the present and the future. Apocalyptic writings often strike us as being intensely pessimistic because the future is viewed as a time of destruction and disaster—a time in which it may appear that God is not in control. Yet, the apocalyptic writer is ever looking beyond that time to when everything will be under God's power.

Signs of the end. In Lesson 6 we left Jesus and His disciples teaching in the temple. Now, the scene shifts. Apparently, after going just a short distance from the temple, they look back at the breathtaking splendor of that magnificent structure. Herod's temple was a dazzling sight, an architectural wonder that dominated the Jerusalem skyline.

After gazing at this familiar yet awesome sight, one of the disciples exclaimed, "Master, see what manner of stones and what buildings are here!" (13:1). Instead of responding with an appropriate comment on their beauty, as we would have, Jesus made a rather startling statement, "Seest thou these great buildings? There shall not be left one stone upon another, that shall not be thrown down" (13:2). This idea seemed ludicrous to the disciples as they stared at the massive stones that were fitted together so perfectly. Indeed, the temple's solid structure gave every appearance of being able to stand until the end of time.

Moving on to the slopes of the Mount of Olives, Jesus and His disciples evidently sat down to talk at a view-point—stretched out below and beyond was the magnificence of the temple and the holy city. It was here that Peter, James, John, and Andrew evidently drew Jesus aside from the rest of the group and asked Him two important questions that referred to His earlier comment about the temple: "When shall these things be?" and "What shall be the sign when all these things shall be fulfilled?" (13:4).

In response to these questions, Jesus clarified His prophetic comments about the temple, by speaking apocalyptically in verses 14–20 of the devastation that would level and lay waste the city of Jerusalem. And in verses 9–13, He warned them of the horrible suffering that Christians would have to endure in the coming years. Then in verses 7 and 8, and 24 through 27, He drew aside the curtain and revealed certain conditions and events that will occur at the time of Jesus' return to earth at the end of the age.

With that in mind, let's examine briefly Jesus' words as He talked with the four disciples. To the ones He had said, "Follow!" Jesus now adds a second command, "Watch!" The discourse itself starts in the middle of 13:5 and occupies the rest of the chapter. Verses 5–23 offer three warnings about signs that point to future events.

First, false messiahs will appear, claiming to be worthy of allegiance. "For many shall come in my name, saying, I am Christ; and shall deceive many" (13:6).

Next, "wars and rumors of wars" will be identified as signs of the end, but Jesus warns against being deceived, for "the end shall not be yet" (13:7).

Third, many natural disasters will occur, such as earthquakes and famine. These, too, are reasons for sorrow, but the context of the passage clearly indicates that they do not mean the End Time has arrived.

Verses 9–13 bring the issue home to Mark's readers. Jesus here reminds His followers that they will be per-

Sustained through trials.

secuted—"delivered up to councils" and beaten in synagogues. The early Christians were, in fact, experiencing such aggrievement, and Jesus' words had the clear and painful ring of reality. From the perspective of the four disciples, the events were yet to come. From the viewpoint of Mark's earliest readers, the persecution had begun.

Note the way Jesus saw trials and tribulations. He viewed them as a means for proclaiming the Good News. Christians used their persecution and even their martyrdom, as a way of testifying to the redeeming power of Christ. When we read about their suffering, we often get the impression that it was those who judged and persecuted them who were on trial—not the Christians. Jesus encouraged His followers to have confidence that the Holy Spirit would sustain and guide them in all kinds of frightening situations: "...take no thought beforehand what ye shall speak, neither do you premeditate: but whatsoever shall be given you in that hour, that speak ye: for it is not ye that speak, but the Holy Ghost" (13:11).

The irony of history is that Christianity was nurtured because of persecution. Christians who fled in fear of their lives became missionaries in new places. Those who suffered and died left an impression of courage and faithfulness that inspired others. No wonder George Bernard Shaw concluded that the best way to stimulate the Christian faith was to feed as many believers as possible to the lions! Mark is calling his readers to endure to the end.

A coming tragedy. Verses 14–23 are hard to understand fully, and most commentators offer only educated guesses, at best, as to their precise meaning. The phrase in verse 14, "the abomination of desolation" has its origin in Daniel 9:27; 11:31; and 12:11. It is generally believed this refers to the pagan pollution of the temple by Antiochus Epiphanes who tried to stamp out the Jewish religion and replace it with Greek thought and customs. He desecrated the temple by offering swine's flesh on the great altar and by setting up brothels in the sacred courts. It is not clear in this verse just what sort of abominable acts were predicted. Perhaps Jesus is referring to some sort of violence that will be done by one of the false messiahs.

Whatever form it took, it would be terrible. Jesus saw the coming tragedy in human terms—the misery caused to farmers working in the fields (13:16) and the pain to

A view of the Wailing Wall or Western Wall in Jerusalem. Massive stones often running from ten to thirty feet in length were a part of the retaining wall around the temple complex. These stones remain from the time of Jesus and are the size and kind referred to by Jesus in Mark 13:1-2.

pregnant women and those with babies (13:17). Verses 15–18 can be understood either as words of warning to Christians in Jerusalem or as a warning about the end of the world. Herod's temple, begun in 20 B.C. and famous for its beauty, was completely destroyed in A.D. 70 as Jesus had predicted, so Mark's readers could have easily connected Jesus' words to this particular event.

Few events in history could match the horror that accompanied the fall of Jerusalem. Titus and his Roman legions laid siege to the city. Over one million people died and almost 100,000 were taken captive. The imagery Jesus used years before this happened was no exaggeration.

Then Jesus again warned His followers to "take heed" and look out for bogus prophets (21–23). Even the most faithful followers can be tempted ("seduced") by false messiahs. His words were true then and continue to be relevant now, for dark times breed those who exploit the fears and miseries of others. The infamous Jim Jones is a

Beware of bogus prophets.

case in point. The people who followed him to their deaths in Guyana were seeking a way out of poverty and misery. Others who shared his cup of poison were idealists disenchanted with the hypocrisy of both the world and the church. The danger was, and is, *real*, and the problem with distinguishing false prophets from true is like choosing between good mushrooms and bad ones. Sometimes we don't know which is which until it is too late.

The coming of the Son of Man.

A shift in the time frame is provided in verse 24: "...in those days, after that tribulation..." In other words, the end of the age will come and all these other troubles—wars, persecutions, famines, false messiahs—will prove to have been just preliminaries. The real End Time will be marked by the coming of the Son of Man.

Verses 24–27 must have been difficult for the early Christians, for their expectation that the end was very near—in their lifetimes—did not come true. These verses are difficult for us, too, and for similar reasons. We are still muddling along, making many mistakes and seeing all the preliminary signs. The earliest Christians may have become impatient as they waited for the Son to come, but we have had many more years of waiting—nearly two thousand—to dampen our sense of expectancy. We have reason to ask even more loudly than first-century Christians, "How much longer?"

As we reread these verses, and review them now as we should, it is helpful to see that in His use of apocalyptic language Jesus has described two events: the fall of Jerusalem in A.D. 70 and the Second Coming of Christ. In responding to the question of the four disciples, He uses the destruction of the temple and the fall of Jerusalem as a springboard to go beyond what they had asked originally—to the End Times. The signs are much the same, and they continue to be. In a real sense, every age is apocalyptic.

As if anticipating our mood, the chapter concludes with two parables that speak to our dilemma. The parable of the fig tree undergirds hope in the coming of the Son of Man and suggests, indeed, that it is an imminent event: "...this generation shall not pass till all these things be done" (13:30). That it didn't happen within the lifetime of Mark is troublesome to us, but, with all its problems, the verse certainly conveys a dramatic sense of urgency.

When connected with the concluding parable of the chapter about the absent master (13:34–37), a universal message for all generations emerges: *be ready.* Here Jesus tells a parable about a man who went on a journey. Before the man left home, he put his servants in charge, each with his own work assignment. He instructed the porter or doorkeeper to be alert, "Watch ye therefore: for ye know not when the master of the house cometh, at even, or at midnight, or at the cockcrowing, or in the morning: lest coming suddenly he find you sleeping" (13:35–36).

This is an important passage, and anyone who considers it irrelevant because Jesus did not return in the first century will miss the larger message—the responsibility to be faithful *now*, to live *as if* Jesus will return tomorrow. This larger message applies to everyone, for life ends with death and this passage of Scripture calls us to be faithful in whatever time we have. It also speaks powerfully to oppressed people, like the slaves in this country who sang, "My Lord, what a morning, when the stars begin to fall!"

A legendary story about Tolstoy, the reknowned Russian writer, makes the point. One day while he was working in his garden, a man approached him and asked, "Sir, what would you do if you suddenly learned you had but one day to live?" Tolstoy replied, "I would continue working in my garden."

His point is clear. Those who live in the present as His faithful disciples, trust that the Son of Man will come again as He promised. They are on watch. They are ready. They do not, at the last minute, need to run around "fixing" their lives should the world—or their lives—end the next day.

So the vision of the future in Chapter 13, as difficult as it is to understand, strengthens discipleship in the present. It warns us against religious phonies who would exploit the dark times of life. It sustains us in whatever persecution we are called to endure. It challenges us to get on with our own proclamations of the gospel. And it reminds us (verse 32) that no one except God knows when the end time will arrive—a timely warning for those who lose valuable time in speculation.

The final days of Jesus' human life are recorded in Mark 14–16. As he has done before, Mark tells one story inside another in the opening verses of Chapter 14. Verses 1–2 and 10–11 sandwich the account of a woman who anoints

The countdown begins.

Jesus at a dinner party. The surrounding verses reveal the plot of the chief priests and scribes to use Judas to seize Jesus at an opportune time. The beauty of the woman's act of anointing Jesus contrasts vividly with the ugliness and hostility of the evil setting.

The collaboration of Judas fits a pattern of misunderstanding and rejection that has characterized Jesus' family, friends, and disciples. Time after time those closest to Jesus have seemed to understand Him less and reject Him more than those who didn't have an intimate relationship with Him. Judas now becomes the extreme example of this irony.

These verses (1–2; 10–11) indicate the reason the chief priests were delighted when Judas went to them with an offer to betray Jesus. They were eager to arrest and prosecute Him, but they were also fearful of the reactions of the crowd. And Jerusalem was jam-packed with pilgrims who had flocked to the holy city to celebrate. The remembrance of their deliverance from Egypt intensified their nationalistic impulses at this time, so any public arrest of Jesus might provoke a riot. Therefore, Judas' offer to help them isolate Jesus and have Him arrested without a public commotion played right into their hands. Now, they could seize Him before the people knew what happened.

This leads us now to an important question: Why did Judas betray Jesus? Thoughtful readers have pondered this question for centuries. Some say Judas betrayed Him for money. Everyone has a price, this line of thinking goes, and Judas had his. Others suggest that Judas wanted to force Jesus to display His divine power. Still other commentators speculate that Judas acted out of intense personal disappointment at Jesus' failure to be the political messiah Judas—and most people—wanted. We don't really know why Judas betrayed Jesus. But his act of betrayal marked his name forever with disgrace and shame.

A celebration of love. While the scribes were collaborating with Judas, Jesus had gone to a dinner party! (14:3–9). It was in the Jerusalem suburb of Bethany at the home of Simon the leper. And while Jesus was eating, "there came a woman having an alabaster box of ointment of spikenard very precious; and she brake the box, and poured it on his head" (14:3).

The woman who anointed Jesus' head is totally anonymous in Mark's Gospel. The "alabaster box of ointment" was probably a vase containing an oil extracted from the nard plant, which is native to India. Appropriately, nard was used for two reasons very different in their purpose: to perfume hair, and to anoint the dead.

But once again those closest to Jesus miss the deeper point of the event as they focus on the obvious. They ask: Why waste the ointment? (14:4). They believed that it could have been used for some practical purpose. Jesus, however, approved of her act because of its timeliness. Jesus knew its symbolism signified His coming death. Further, it was a selfless act of love. Jesus understood this and honored her for it, "Let her alone; why trouble ye her? She hath wrought a good work on me" (14:6).

Children often do kindnesses without considering the sacrifice involved. A child may spend her entire allowance to buy perfume for her mother, without thinking that she spent "too much." Or we take flowers to a dying friend, not because it is sensible to do so, but because we care.

However, the story of this woman in no way justifies ignoring the needs of the poor. Jesus' whole ministry rebuts that argument. It is, instead, an example of love that is spontaneous and sacrificial. There are times when we need to celebrate our love in extravagant or even foolish ways.

The Last Supper.

The countdown continues. Mark says in 14:12 that "on the first day of unleavened bread," the disciples asked about Jesus' plans for celebrating the Passover meal. Evidently Jesus had already made arrangements with some friends, and now He sent two disciples ahead to complete preparations. There was nothing haphazard about the plan. Jesus told His disciples to look for a man carrying a pitcher of water and to follow him. For us, this might seem like a risky means of identification. But carrying a water pitcher was something a man wouldn't normally do because that was woman's work. There was probably only one such man in all the city, so the disciples had no trouble locating him. They followed him and when he arrived at a certain house, he went in. They then spoke to the owner, saying, "The Master saith where is the guest chamber" where Jesus and His disciples shall eat the Passover? In response to what was apparently a prearranged signal, the owner took them to an upper room where they made the necessary preparations.

Verse 17 marks a shift in time and place. It is evening and they are all gathered in the upper room to share the Passover meal. While they eat, Jesus makes a startling announcement, "One of you which eateth with me shall betray me" (14:18). Each one questioned Jesus, "Is it I?" No one had any idea that it was Judas.

Jesus did, of course, but He does not reveal the name of the betrayer to others. It was as if Jesus were letting Judas be responsible for his own deeds, for surely the other disciples would have prevented Judas from acting had they known his intentions.

The Passover meal that night became what we know as the Last Supper, and it provided a symbolic summary of what had been unfolding in the life of Jesus. In that meal we have the theme of *sacrifice*: "This is my body... This is my blood." There is the message of *atonement*: "This is my blood of the new testament which is shed for many." And there is the promise of a *reunion* with Jesus in a joyous fellowship beyond the cross: "I will drink no more of the fruit of the vine, until that day that I drink it new in the Kingdom of God" (14:25). No wonder the early church made the Last Supper a sacrament. Jesus in that final Passover meal was doing symbolically what He was going to do the next day.

There is no doubt that the love and affection shared that night by Jesus and His closest followers was genuine. When Jesus handed the cup to His disciples, it symbolized the life and suffering they were to share. When the meal was concluded, Mark tells us that "when they had sung an hymn, they went out into the Mount of Olives" (14:26).

In spite of His disciples' love for Him, however, Jesus knew He would soon be alone. He knew that all of them, not just Judas, would fall away, for He told them that they would "be offended," which means to "stumble over an obstacle," or "fall into a trap." Of all the pain Jesus was to endure, none was greater than the realization that He would be abandoned by all. The shepherd would die and the sheep would be scattered (14:27).

Impetuous Peter would have none of this kind of talk, however. He vehemently contradicted Jesus with a vow, "Although all shall be offended, yet will not I" (14:29). The others chimed in, adding their own protestations of loyalty. But Jesus knew better, and He confronted Peter eyeball to eyeball, "Verily I say unto thee, that this day, even in this night, before the cock crow twice, thou shall deny me thrice" (14:30).

While the phrase "cock crow" may have referred to the early morning crowing of a rooster, probably it was instead a reference to the Roman trumpet call announcing the beginning of the fourth watch at 3:00 A.M. A bugle call always announced the changing of the guard, and this was referred to as the "cockcrow." Jesus told Peter that before the fourth watch began, he would deny Him three times.

In the Garden.

No scene in the New Testament captures both the humanity and the divinity of Jesus as fully as that in the Garden of Gethsemane. The drama has narrowed, so that Jesus was alone with His three most trusted disciples. Peter, James, and John, who have just declared their absolute loyalty to Jesus, fall asleep when Jesus asks them to stand watch while He prays. After spending time alone in agonizing prayer, Jesus returned to where the disciples were waiting and found them asleep. Jesus then said to Peter, "Simon, sleepest thou? Couldest not thou watch one

A rock outcropping in the Garden of Gethsemane. According to tradition, this is the stone on which Jesus prayed in His agony. It now forms a part of the altar of a modern church.

hour?" (14:37). Note that Jesus uses the name "Simon," as calling the sleeping disciple by his new name, "Peter" or "rock," was certainly inappropriate now. Already they had fulfilled His prediction of falling away by falling asleep. This same scene was enacted two more times.

But back to Jesus' prayer. It demonstrated two things: human agony and divine faithfulness. He knew without doubt that His death was within the will of God, but that knowledge did not temper His intense feelings of abandonment, anguish, and sorrow. Jesus had no martyr complex. There is no indication at this point that He faced death serenely, and His human anguish enables us to comprehend something of the pain of that moment. Actually, a more literal translation of what Jesus experienced is, "He began to be terrified and disoriented." Out of the deep distress of His soul Jesus used the Aramaic phrase for "father," which is *abba*. It connotes the more informal "daddy." From this we can conclude that Jesus is in the situation of a helpless child who recognizes his helplessness and cries out, "Daddy!"

At this point Jesus had every reason to run for His life. Instead, though, He returned to where His disciples were sleeping and said, "Rise up, let us go; lo, he that betrayeth me is at hand" (14:42).

The arrest.   Suddenly the action shifts from a lonely struggle to a mob scene. Judas comes into the Garden leading a pack of authorities who were carrying swords and staves. Following through with his prearranged identification signal, Judas approaches Jesus, "and saith Master, master and kissed him" (14:45). And with that, Jesus is arrested on the spot. It is interesting to note here that the word Mark uses for "kiss" connotes intimacy; it means to kiss as a lover kisses his beloved. It was customary to greet a rabbi with a kiss. To do so was merely a sign of respect and affection. A lover's kiss, however, adds a note of poignancy to this scene.

Jesus' response to the arrest is that of fearless human dignity. A few minutes before, alone in the Garden, He had poured out His soul to God. Now in the face of a hostile mob, His quiet courage provides a model for everyone of all time who may face persecution.

Next, Jesus asks the obvious question that exposes the crowd's cowardice, "Are ye come out, as against a thief, with swords and with staves to take me? I was daily with you in the temple teaching, and ye took me not" (14:48–49). Cowards run in packs and do their worst under cover of darkness.

In contrast to Jesus' quiet courage, the disciples panicked. "One of them that stood by" drew a sword and cut off the ear of a servant of the high priest (14:47), but Mark does not elaborate on the incident, and the impression is left that it was an ineffectual, meaningless gesture. Next, Mark tells us that in their fright "they all forsook him and fled." Mark also records the story of a young man who was so frightened, he ran away literally without his clothes. Now Jesus is left to walk the lonesome road alone.

After taking Jesus captive and directing Him to the high priest's palace, the chief priests, elders, and scribes gathered in an official, if irregular, meeting of the Sanhedrin, the highest Jewish council. It was "official" in the sense that legal vocabulary was used, i.e. words like witness, testimony, and condemned. Also, some judicial procedures were followed: two witnesses were sought to provide common testimony. But the "trial" was irregular, to say the least, because the verdict was pre-determined (14:55) and the evidence was false (14:56,57,59). Any semblance of fair play was absent. The Sanhedrin that night was a kangaroo court.

A kangaroo court.

The religious authorities, however, got what they wanted. In examining Jesus, the high priest asked Him a leading question, "Art thou the Christ, the Son of the Blessed?" (14:61). Time after time, as we have seen, Jesus outwitted His opponents whenever they sought to catch Him in an incriminating response. This moment, however, is the moment of truth. It is time to be done with the whole dirty business. Jesus' Messiahship is no longer a secret to be gradually revealed. His death is certain, whatever His answer to the question. So He replies, "I am, and ye shall see the Son of man sitting on the right hand of power, and coming in the clouds of heaven" (14:62). His answer enrages the high priest who tears his clothes and exclaims that Jesus has blasphemed.

The Jewish leaders finally had the "confession" they wanted. To claim to be the Messiah was one charge they could pass on with some clout to the Roman court. The fact that Jesus meant something entirely different by the word

A dungeon prison beneath the Church of St. Peter in Gallicantu, Jerusalem. This is considered the probable site of the House of Caiaphas and is likely the prison area where Jesus was held overnight prior to His crucifixion.

than the military figure the Romans feared was irrelevant. The mob took over and slapped Jesus, spat on Him, and ridiculed Him. Jesus' physical torment had begun.

Peter's denial.

In the meantime, though, Peter, as verse 54 shows, had slipped inside the palace courtyard where he stood furtively around a fire with servants. To his credit he had not run into hiding like the rest of the disciples, and he may have inwardly clung to the belief that he would be faithful to the end.

The account of Peter's denial had special meaning for early Christians who read it in Mark's Gospel. They, too, were continually being tested in courts and, more often, in the common dialogues of life. The accusation brought three times against Peter is that he was "with Jesus of Nazareth"—guilty by association.

In three stages Peter caved in. First, he pleaded ignorance, "I know not, neither understand I what thou sayest" (14:68). Next, he disclaimed being one of Jesus' disciples—when a maid said, "This is one of them." A third time he was accused, by virtue of his Galilaean speech, of being a follower of Jesus. This time Peter's denial was accompanied by cursing. He denied Jesus himself, "I know not this man of whom ye speak" (14:71).

Then the bugle sounded. The "cockcrowing" reminded Peter that Jesus' prediction had come to pass. And the pain of what he had done drove him to tears. Had Paul Harvey, the radio commentator been describing the event, he might have said, "...and now we have the rest of the story."

And yet we don't. Peter's denial was reported by Mark, and there is good reason to believe that Mark got the story indirectly from Peter himself. Peter's story, however, doesn't end with his denial, for he went on to become the "rock" Jesus called him to be.

Like Peter, we also claim our undying loyalty to Christ, and the bugle calls of personal security remind us of our denials. For the first-century Christians to whom Mark wrote, Peter's denial was a warning and a promise. They—and we—are warned that to identify with Christ and His church is to invite possible death, and denial is always a temptation. But all of us who are Christian are left with the promise that Christ will be with us when the question comes, "Are you one of His disciples?" To say "yes," even today, requires courage and the help of Christ.

Your profound suffering emanates from these pages. Thank You, Lord, for giving of Yourself on Calvary that we might have life. AMEN.

WHAT THIS SCRIPTURE MEANS TO ME
—Mark 14:1–15:15

"A friend is someone who likes me even though she knows me!"

"...there is a friend that sticketh closer than a brother" (Prov. 18:24).

"A friend loveth at all times" (Prov. 17:17).

These three familiar sayings give us a word picture of a particular kind of friend—one who is close, faithful, and supportive.

"My friends scorn me: but mine eye poureth out tears to God" (Job 16:20).

"My friends stand aloof from my sore" (Psa. 38:11).

On the other hand, these two biblical references seem to give us a completely different word picture. Here are so-called friends who are not faithful to the relationship and are not supportive.

But even with true friendship there are different levels. Some people are acquaintances. These are people we know slightly or casually. We wave at them across the fence or chat briefly with them at the store or nod to them at church. Actually, we know little about them except what is public information.

A second level of friendship takes the relationship a little deeper. This involves occasional social contacts—visits in one another's homes or dinner together at a favorite restaurant. At this level we know more about our friends—their likes, dislikes; their family story.

It is interesting, though, that neither of the above two levels call for a particular commitment—either party could likely back off gracefully without leaving hurt feelings if there didn't seem to be enough in common to nurture a deeper relationship.

And then, of course, there is that third level of friendship in which a genuine and healthy intimacy develops. In a relationship of this kind we can be vulnerable with each other—completely ourselves without fear of being judged. This kind of friendship is built on mutual trust; it involves sharing our deepest feelings and fondest hopes openly with another person. Friendship of this kind and quality is one of our greatest treasures.

I believe it was this deep level of friendship Jesus had with His disciples. They had lived and traveled together for over three years. Undoubtedly, they had laughed together over the joys in their journeys. And, undoubtedly, they had cried together as they felt the pain and hurt of people with their physical and emotional suffering. And in their quiet times together it is very likely that they shared their deepest feelings—their hopes and dreams.

And yet, there are three poignant scenes in our lesson that underline the fragility of even the kind of intimacy that existed between such good friends as Jesus and the twelve disciples.

In the first scene Jesus asks three of His closest friends, Peter, James, and John to stand watch with Him while He prays. Jesus knows His death is just hours away, and in these moments of trial and agony He wants and needs the support of friends. But instead they fell asleep.

The second scene has Judas betraying his friend. After over three years of intimate friendship, Judas places a kiss on Jesus' cheek signaling to the police that He was their man. Matthew tells us that even here Jesus called Judas, "Friend."

The third scene takes us to the palace of the high priest. Jesus has been arrested and is standing trial inside before the Sanhedrin. Outside in the courtyard, Peter, Jesus' closest friend, is asked three times if he isn't one of Jesus' disciples. But each time Peter denies that he even knows Jesus. Imagine!

Most of us at various times, I'm sure, have felt let down by a friend or betrayed or denied. At such moments the hurt is deep and there is the temptation to strike back or become bitter. But this is not the model of behavior Jesus gives us. Instead, with singleness of purpose He moved on in love to die for those who might betray Him or deny Him or go to sleep on Him.

The Scripture verses in this lesson carry many different meanings for me. But as I reflect on them again, the importance of friendship, of being a faithful friend, has impressed me as never before. John put it this way, "Greater love hath no man than this, that a man lay down his life for his friends" (John 15:13).

LESSON 8
MARK 15:1–16:20

The End of the Beginning

Lord, let the truths in this lesson grip my heart and spirit. AMEN.

The morning after Jesus' arrest He appeared once more before the Sanhedrin. The farcial "trial" that had been held a few hours before had happened after sunset and was unofficial because of Jewish law. But now they met to confirm the charge of blasphemy, and, more importantly, to haul Jesus off to Pilate, the Roman governor. It was not within the Sanhedrin's power to put Him to death, therefore, they sought to establish a charge of treason based on His claim to be king of the Jews, and to convince Pilate that He was a threat to Roman law and order (15:1).

Jesus before Pilate.   Jesus' trial before Pilate parallels His appearance before the Sanhedrin. During both trials He was interrogated, condemned, and mocked. All of the action occurred at the Roman governor's official residence, the Praetorium. Mark wanted his readers to see that there was ample blame to go around. Both religious and civil authorities were responsible for Jesus' death. Jesus was rejected first by Jerusalem and then by Rome. Mark, by implication, adds a third party to the crime, the crowd, which intimidated Pilate into deciding to release Barabbas rather than Jesus.

The interrogation of Jesus by Pilate featured a different question from that which the high priest had asked Him the night before. Jesus had boldly answered "yes" to

The Pilate inscription. This stone was found at Caesarea and refers to the reign of Tiberius and contains the name of Pontius Pilate, prefect of the province of Judea. When this was found, it was the first definitive evidence discovered in Palestine of the governorship of Pilate.

Caiaphas' earlier question, "Art thou the Christ, the Son of the Blessed?" (15:2). But Pilate's question was, "Art thou the king of the Jews?" The Roman governor wanted to know if Jesus was a revolutionary, a fanatic seeking to overthrow the civil government.

Jesus' answer to Pilate was evasive, "Thou sayest it." It was as if Jesus said, "You know very well I am no political revolutionary. My kingdom is based on love." Jesus knew the charges were fabricated and the trial was a charade. And He knew that Pilate was also aware of the game being played.

At His appearance before Pilate, the chief priests spilled their venom, but Jesus' reply was louder than all their accusations: silence. There was nothing more to be said, and Pilate was amazed at Jesus' aloofness—we would call it "cool"—in the face of their vehemence (15:4–5).

The character of Pontius Pilate is displayed in Mark's brief account of this event. The historical record shows that Pilate was the Roman Procurator of Judea during A.D. 26–36. He had deep contempt, generally, for the people he ruled. He crushed riots mercilessly and often ordered executions. The chief priests, in handing Jesus over to Pilate, knew they had an excellent chance of succeeding in their efforts to eliminate this Galilean troublemaker. Today, Pilate would be known as a "hanging judge."

Mark's account of the trial reveals two contrasting attitudes in Pilate. He was obviously impressed by Jesus, and his offer to release a prisoner was a way out of his predicament. The last thing Pilate wanted was trouble with the thousands of people who had traveled to Jerusalem for the Passover, so he tried to get off the hook by offering to release Jesus.

In any other circumstances Jesus would have been the better choice for release over Barabbas, an insurgent rebel who was sitting on death row (15:7). But when Pilate suggested that Jesus be released, according to the custom of the time, the chief priests incited the crowd to ask for Barabbas' release instead (15:11). He then asked, "What will ye then that I shall do unto him whom ye call the King of the Jews?" And with that the frenzied mob shouted "Crucify him!" Pilate then surrendered to their demands "and delivered Jesus, when he had scourged him, to be crucified," (15:15).

Pilate knew Jesus was innocent, but his weak, vacillating behavior on this day has caused him to be remembered forever as the prime example of selfish ambition and moral flab. For this small-time bureaucrat, it was all in a day's work. The irony is that this was Pilate's only claim to fame, for his decision has been recorded forever in the Apostle's Creed: "...suffered under Pontius Pilate."

Scourging and mocking. Mark 15:15 says that Pilate turned Jesus over after he had "scourged him." That one word describes a tortuous process known and feared by all who lived under Roman justice. The scourge was a leather thong studded with pieces of lead and bone. When a prisoner was whipped with a scourge, his body was subjected to horrible torture.

In addition to the custom of whipping prisoners before they were executed, the Roman soldiers mocked them unmercifully. Jesus was treated like any other condemned man and became the helpless victim of their cruel horseplay. They dressed Him in royal purple, put a crown of thorns on His head, and shouted, "Hail, King of the Jews." Treating someone about to be executed as if he were a king was the sickest of sick jokes.

Evil is always heightened when its perpetrators add their mocking laughter. In the movie, "The Ipcress File," one scene pictures the careful and deliberate execution of several Jewish prisoners by a Nazi officer. One by one he methodically shoots prisoners in the head so that they fall backwards into graves they had dug for themselves. At one point, instead of shooting a young boy who stands resigned to his fate, he fires into the air. The boy, in a reflex action, falls into his grave. The Nazi officers laugh lustily when he staggers to his feet, bewildered and terrified, uncertain as to what has happened. With the laughter of his captors ringing in his ears, he is then shot. The mocking of Jesus was cruel punishment and, psychologically, the painful equivalent of another scourging.

Jesus' own prediction and Old Testament prophecy had both come to pass. His persecution was a vivid reminder to Mark's first-century readers of their own suffering for the faith. And from the time Jesus answered Pilate's question until He was nearly dead on the cross, Jesus uttered no recorded words in the Gospel of Mark. Yet the faithful saw in the quiet figure of Jesus the real king.

By their action the chief priests, the mob, Pilate, and the soldiers condemned themselves. Real authority rested with Jesus, for He was more than a noble example or an innocent sufferer. Jesus represented the authority of God Himself.

The crucifixion, toward which Mark's entire Gospel builds, is described in only twenty-one verses (15:21–41). Indeed, all of Chapter fifteen has been summarized in four affirmations from the Apostle's Creed. Jesus suffered under Pontius Pilate (verses 1–20), was crucified (verses 21–32), dead (33–41), and buried (42–47). The key event in Christian history on which Christ's resurrection turns is treated by Mark in a graphic but succinct manner.

The crucifixion.

Simon the Cyrenian made a brief appearance in verse 21, establishing a claim to history as the one who carried Jesus' cross. Jesus was evidently so weakened by the scourging that He was not strong enough to carry His cross Himself. So Simon, a passerby, was drafted for the dishonorable task (15:21). There is no reason to suppose that Simon had ever met Jesus before that day. He was probably one of the pilgrims in Jerusalem for Passover. Mark assumed however, that his readers would identify

The Via Dolorosa in Jerusalem, the traditional route Jesus went as He carried His cross on the way to Calvary.

Simon by his children, Alexander and Rufus, who evidently were well known in the early church. It is possible that Rufus was the same person Paul referred to in Romans 16:13, "Salute Rufus chosen in the Lord, and his mother and mine." Possibly Simon and his family joined the Christian movement because he was forced, that fateful day, to carry the cross of Jesus.

Mark then went on to say that they brought Jesus to Golgotha, which means "the place of the skull" (15:22). One reason it may have been given that macabre name was that prisoners often took a long time to die, and some of them became prey for vultures and wild dogs after they were removed from their crosses. There were probably several

Gordon's Calvary. A rocky outcropping just north of the city of Jerusalem with pockmarks creating the impression of a skull. This has been identified as the probable Place of the Skull, or the site of the crucifixion of Jesus.

skulls and other parts of human skeletons in the area— grim reminders of what happened regularly on Golgotha.

Next, they offered Jesus "wine mingled with myrrh," but He would not drink it (15:23). Merciful women present at crucifixions sometimes gave criminals a drink of drugged wine to ease the terrible pain. Jesus, however, chose to meet His death with His senses intact. His pain was not dulled by an anesthetic.

Our ability to comprehend the cruelty and pain of crucifixion has dulled over the years by reducing the cross to a piece of jewelry or a shiny symbol. As a means of execution, however, it was unmatched for its ability to prolong death while extending human suffering.

Prisoners were affixed to the "T" shaped cross while it

was lying on the ground. Their hands were nailed to each end of the cross bar, and their feet were bound together to the upright post. Then the cross was lifted up and shoved into a hole in the ground. There they were left to hang until they died. Often a prisoner would go insane before death brought relief.

The cross and cruelty were synonymous, and the death of Jesus occurred at a time in history when crucifixion was the worst possible way to die.

While Jesus was hanging on the cross, the soldiers gambled for His clothes (15:24). The soldiers were probably the four who had accompanied Jesus and Simon to Golgotha. One of the "perks" for doing their duty was to get the criminal's clothes. Some articles, for example, the robe, were more valuable than others, so they gambled for each bit of clothing.

Mark tells us that two thieves were crucified at the same time as Jesus, one on either side of Him. While executing prisoners in groups was commonplace, Mark reminds his readers that this, too, was evidence that Scripture was being fulfilled: "And the scripture was fulfilled, which saith, And he was numbered with the transgressors" (15:27–28). The reference here is to the prophecy in Isaiah 53:12.

It is difficult for any modern reader to imagine the scene that was typical during a crucifixion. Passersby ridiculed Jesus, mocked Him, and hurled insults. Mark reports some of the phrases that were hurled at Jesus in derision, "Ah, thou that destroyest the temple, and buildest it in three days, save thyself and come down from the cross" (15:29–30). The chief priests gloated to the scribes, "He saved others; himself he cannot save. Let Christ the King of Israel descend now from the cross, that we may see and believe" (15:31–32). Even the other two prisoners being crucified with Jesus ridiculed Him, the ultimate insult.

Mark understood what the spectators at the crucifixion did not. As General Booth, a founder of the Salvation Army, observed, "It is because Jesus did not come down from the cross that we believe in Him." No cross, no crown.

The drama of Jesus' crucifixion is heightened by Mark's noting of the times during the Roman day when certain events occurred. In verse 25 he reports that it was the third hour when they crucified Him. Later, in verse 33, he tells us that from "the sixth hour, there was darkness over the whole land until the ninth hour." By our reckoning of time, then, Jesus' crucifixion began at 9:00 in the morning, and the skies were dark between noon and 3:00 p.m. The darkness underscored the tragic significance of Jesus' death. It was, indeed, a black day in history.

At the ninth hour (3:00 p.m.) Mark reports that Jesus cried out in Aramaic the words that have troubled many Christians for generations, "My God, my God, why hast thou forsaken me?" (15:34). Jesus' cry is a direct quotation of Psalm 22:1 and has come to be known as "the cry of desolation." Martin Luther was among those troubled by this verse. "God, forsaken by God!" he said. "How can it be?"

There is a mystery for us in these dying words of Jesus. But as the sinless Jesus felt the full burden of the sin of the human race, He experienced something He had never known before—separation from God. Now He felt in His own being the results of sin.

Certain of the bystanders mistook the cry of "Eloi, Eloi" for the name of Elijah and thought Jesus was calling for help. Someone else filled a sponge with vinegar—sour wine—and put it on a reed and offered it to Jesus to drink. It was undoubtedly not a compassionate act, for Mark suggests it was done only to keep Jesus' dehydrated body alive a little while longer so they could "see whether Elias will come to take him down" (15:36).

With another great cry, Jesus died. As crucifixions went, it was a fairly quick death. And simultaneously with Jesus' last breath, the curtain of the temple was "rent in twain from the top to the bottom" (15:38). To Mark's earliest readers the tearing of the curtain meant one of two things. It was either a symbol of the destruction of Jewish religion and the temple itself, or it represented the final breakdown of the barriers between the presence of God and humanity.

Jesus' death.

The curtain in the temple served to shut off the Holy of Holies, where God was present in a special way, out of the congregation's view. Only the priest had ever been allowed to enter this holy place. But now this dividing curtain was useless. Through Jesus' death the Holy of Holies was now open to all people in all time.

Most of the people clustered around the cross that day were apparently unmoved by Jesus' death. They were callous and cynical to the end. One exception was the centurion, a Roman military officer on duty at the cross. The effect on him was life-changing, and Mark reported his words as if they were a confession of faith, "Truly this man was the Son of God" (15:39). But the gentile soldier, like most of Mark's readers, was able to see the truth only after Jesus had died.

Now the "secret" of the Gospel has come full circle. Mark announced in his first verse (1:1) who Jesus was, recorded Peter's confession in the middle of his Gospel (8:29), and climaxed the death of Jesus by reporting the words of the Roman centurion.

Mark then tells us that certain women were distant spectators to the crucifixion events, Mary Magdalene; Mary, the mother of James and John; and Salome. No mention is made of the disciples who had declared absolute loyalty to Jesus. James and John were not there, but their mother was. So were "many other women which came up with him into Jerusalem" (15:41). I believe this information is significant because it confirms the essential role women played in the beginnings of the Christian movement.

The burial. Although Mark is customarily very economical with words, he spares nothing in giving us a careful description of Jesus' burial. First he introduces Joseph of Arimathea as "an honorable, counsellor," a respected member of the council. He then tells us that Joseph "also waited for the kingdom of God" (15:43).

Joseph was not a member of the inner circle of disciples—they had all taken off and were long gone. But we read that he "went in boldly to Pilate" and asked for the body of Jesus. This called for rare courage on Joseph's part. He risked his standing to do what he believed to be right.

In verse 44 Mark tells us that Pilate was surprised to hear that Jesus was already dead, so he checked with the centurion on duty. And when it was confirmed by the officer, he gave Joseph permission to take Jesus' body. This was the equivalent to issuing a death certificate.

Mark now continues his careful description of what happened next. Joseph took Jesus' body down from the cross and wrapped it in fine linen. The body was then placed in the sepulchre, and a heavy stone was rolled over the opening to prevent desecration by animals or grave robbers. Mark then tells that this entire scene was witnessed by Mary Magdalene and Mary the mother of Joses.

The Garden Tomb. This ancient tomb was found in a garden adjacent to Gordon's Calvary. It was hewn out of rock and contained a channel for a rolling or closing stone in front of it. Crosses painted on the wall of the tomb indicate its importance in early Christianity. According to much tradition, it is the burial site of Jesus.

There is great significance for us in Mark's descriptive account. Joseph, a member of the Jewish council, the Roman governor, the soldier on watch at the cross, and the Galilean women all knew that Jesus was dead and buried. Mark thereby underscored one essential fact: Jesus really died and was really buried. Any claims that He recovered or was resuscitated simply do not square with Mark's account. Heresies that denied the physical death of Jesus would be rejected by careful readers of Mark's Gospel. If Jesus were known to be alive after Easter day, it had to be by resurrection from the dead.

The women of the Gospel story were last at the cross and first at the tomb. Three faithful women played a striking role in discovering and announcing the resurrection of Jesus. "And when the Sabbath was past, Mary Magdalene, and Mary the mother of James, and Salome, had brought spices, that they might come and anoint him" (16:1). For women to play such a prominent role was shocking, given their low status in Jewish society. Among Jews, no woman's testimony was trusted in court, so it is re-

The empty tomb.

markable that Mark unhesitatingly reports that women were the first witnesses to the empty tomb (16:2–4).

The three women did not go to the tomb that morning with any expectations other than to anoint Jesus' body, a service roughly comparable to embalming. They fully expected to find a corpse in the sealed tomb, and their major concern was how to roll away the stone that sealed the entrance of the sepulchre. But, instead, they found an open grave, and the body of Jesus was missing. "A young man," Mark reports, was "sitting on the right side, clothed in a long white garment" (16:5). His presence frightened them.

Who the "young man" was is less important than what he said, "Be not affrightened. Ye seek Jesus of Nazareth, which was crucified: he is risen; he is not here; behold the place where they laid him" (16:6). The words are partly a reproof, and the young man—or angel—is mildly rebuking the women for failing to believe Jesus' promise that God would raise Him from the dead. The message dramatically reverses the tragedy, which had seemed to end in the abandonment and death of Jesus. Looking among the dead for the crucified Jesus, the women were told, was futile.

Then the women received specific instructions, "...go your way, tell his disciples and Peter that he goeth before you into Galilee: there ye shall see him, as he said unto you" (16:7). This was a reminder of what Jesus had told them in 14:28, "After I am risen, I will go before you into Galilee." Galilee was the place from which the disciples and the women had come. It was their home turf, and now it represented the jumping off place for the great missionary task which awaited Jesus' followers.

The rest of the story. Interpreters of Mark's Gospel have long speculated over the idea that his account actually ended with verse 8. The reasons for this are not particularly important to us as we study this lesson. It is obvious at this point that we are not "at the end of the story." So we will continue on with the concluding verses as we have them in the King James Version.

Following the happenings in the tomb, the women fled in astonishment and fear. In fact, Mark says they were so afraid they didn't tell anyone what had happened. Their eyes were closed to the wonder of Jesus' resurrection.

Next, in verses 9–14, we have the brief report of three post-resurrection appearances of Jesus. First, He appeared to Mary Magdalene. Unlike the other women, she told the disciples, but they refused to believe her (16:9–11).

Jesus' second appearance was to two of the other disciples as they were walking in the country. But, again, when these two told the others, they refused to believe. And finally Jesus appeared to all eleven disciples while they were eating (16:14). And Mark tells us here that Jesus "upbraided them with their unbelief and hardness of heart, because they believed not them which had seen him after he was risen."

Jesus then goes on in verses 15–18 to give the eleven disciples His final instructions. They are to preach the Good News of the gospel to *everyone,* and then He mentions certain signs that accompany the commission. The picturesque language used here is difficult for us to understand in our day. But the important message for us is this: Jesus commissioned His disciples and us to take the salvation message, validated by His death and resurrection, to our family, our neighbors, and people everywhere. And He assured them and us that He will give us the power to carry out the sacred task.

We know from other parts of the gospel story that the followers of Jesus were transformed from fearful cowards after the arrest and crucifixion of Jesus into bold and fearless proclaimers of salvation through Christ. After their empowerment at Pentecost, they moved out across the world

The Chapel of the Ascension is located at the top of the Mount of Olives. This chapel identifies the traditional site from which Jesus ascended into heaven after His crucifixion, resurrection, and appearances to His disciples.

133

witnessing to the resurrection of Jesus, and they did it with power. They brought the New Testament and the early church into existence through their proclamation of the resurrection of Jesus—the central affirmation of Christianity.

Mark affirms all of this in the closing two verses of his Gospel as he speaks of Jesus' ascension to heaven (16:19) and then says, "They went forth, and preached everywhere, the Lord working with them, and confirming the word with signs following" (16:20).

Here, too, we find our source of power today—*the Lord working with us.* With this confidence we can say "Amen" in agreement with the closing word of the Gospel lesson.

Lord, Your profound suffering is surpassed only by Your victory over the grave. And I have victory over death because You do! AMEN.

WHAT THIS SCRIPTURE MEANS TO ME
—Mark 15:16—16:20

Most everyone loves the springtime. The air is fresh and clear, and flowers of every kind pack carefully cared-for beds. The grass is a rich green; the shrubs and trees are sending out new shoots and leaves. Even in the milder parts of our country where I have lived for so many years, spring is a joy, an announcement that life is renewing itself.

It's a great time to stroll in the park, work in the yard, hike in the mountains, or meander down a country lane. Winter is over, and all of nature seems glad. And I'm always glad; there's a new bounce in my step.

But then I'm reminded that without winter there wouldn't be any spring. For so much of nature, winter is a time of death—the trees lose their leaves, grass turns brown and seems lifeless, flowers fade and die, even certain animals go into long hibernation. In some parts of our country the weather turns cooler and in other parts it gets really cold, with snow and ice.

For many, especially where the winters are harsh, winter, like death, is a time of grieving. It's something to be endured, a cycle to go through in order to experience the promise of the coming spring. Northern winters, with their piercing winds, snow-covered landscape, and bleak, leafless trees, are indeed a reminder of death. But with unquestioned certainty we can always know that in time the glory of spring will follow the darkness of winter. It is the hope of spring that makes the winters of our lives bearable, for out ahead we know there will be new life as nature is resurrected into an explosion of beauty.

What a beautiful metaphor of the death and resurrection of Jesus in our lesson! As we have moved through the Gospel of Mark and have seen the buildup of controversy and conflict, the storm clouds of winter have been building up on the horizon. And then the drama moves, with all of its bleakness and stormy violence to Jesus' arrest, trial, and crucifixion. By mid-afternoon Jesus is dead, taken down from the cross, and laid away in a tomb—a cave in the ground. Everything seems as hopeless as a bleak winter landscape. There's no sign of life; it is a picture of death; the tree of life seems to have lost its leaves.

But then something happens. Out of death comes life. When the two Marys and Salome went to the tomb on that first Easter morning, they were told "he is risen; he is not here." This was shocking news to them. They were familiar with the cycles of winter, spring, summer, and fall. However, this was something entirely different for them.

But we understand! How wonderful and thoughtful of God to plan for the resurrection of His Son in the springtime of the year! For it was on that first Easter morning that Jesus, in conquering death and the grave, brought to you and me the opportunity of living eternally in the springtime of His love.

For me, the death and resurrection of Jesus is the source of two promises that are life-changing. First, we have the promise of new life in Christ *now*. Paul drives this point home in 2 Corinthians when he says, "...if any man be in Christ, he is a new creature: old things are passed away; behold, all things are become new" (5:17). For the Christian there shouldn't be dull, drab, or routine days. Every new day is a resurrection—a time of fresh opportunities in our lives for the Lord. As the Psalmist awakened to the joy of a new day, he expressed it beautifully when he wrote, "This is the day which the Lord hath made; we will rejoice and be glad in it" (Psa. 118:24).

And then we have the promise of new life *forever*. The resurrection of Jesus brought us the assurance that He has the power over death. In Him, there is eternal life beyond the grave for the Christian. Paul could hardly contain his joy over the realization of this truth as he wrote, "For this corruptible must put on incorruption, and this mortal must put on immortality. So when this corruptible shall have put on incorruption, and this mortal shall have put on immortality, then shall be brought to pass the saying that is written, Death is swallowed up in victory...thanks be to God which giveth us the victory through our Lord Jesus Christ" (1 Cor. 15:53—57).

Jesus is the guarantee that what God said, He would do. His resurrection from the dead is that proof.

The Twelve Disciples of Jesus

The warm, vulnerable humanity of the Twelve Disciples reaches across the centuries. They were not figures in stained glass windows, with bright, shining halos, nor were they lifeless statues with glittering, gilded robes, and empty eyes that gazed soulfully heavenward. Instead, they were real people, with tears, and smiles, and sometimes muddy feet.

The Disciples' diverse appeal forms a wonderful bridge between us and the perfection of the Lord. I believe part of the reason Jesus selected those particular men was that ordinary folk could identify with them.

When they were called to follow Him not one of them was noted for genius, prestige, or power. Their lovable, admirable qualities, as well as their failings and weaknesses, are common to everyone. We see them in our neighbors, friends, loved ones, and ourselves.

Yet, despite the betrayal of our Lord by Judas Iscariot, the remaining eleven made an impact on the world that changed the course of history.

That governors, kings, and even the vicious Roman Emperor, Nero, should fear and seek to destroy them is remarkable. They were neither wealthy nor a military threat. There is no evidence that any of them had an impressive physical appearance. Even their skills in speaking and writing were negligible, for they were unsophisticated, with little education. Indeed, all they had was their relationship with a man named Jesus.

Overcoming the most terrible persecutions and difficulties, these wonderful, warm and intensely human men established the Christian Church for the ages to come. Tradition holds that it cost most of them their lives.

As we consider each of them, we cannot help but sense that because of their witness, their indefatigable labors, and their courage, we who are Christians owe them an enormous debt.

SIMON PETER

The warmth of Simon Peter's personality spills from the Gospel pages. He was big-hearted, volatile, impetuous, enthusiastic.

Originally from Bethsaida, on the Sea of Galilee, Peter worked as a fisherman in partnership with his brother Andrew and his father Jona. We know that he was married because Jesus healed his wife's mother (Matt. 8:14–15; Mark 1:29–31; Luke 4:38–39). With prophetic foresight, Jesus changed his name from Simon to Peter, meaning "Rock."

He swiftly emerged as the leader of the disciples. Throughout the Gospels, Peter's leadership role is emphasized. Repeatedly, he is noted as the spokesman for the group.

His gifted answer to Jesus' question at Caesarea Philippi, "Whom say ye that I am?" rings through the ages. Today, no matter what our denomination, at the very foundation, at rock center, we share Peter's response, "Thou art the Christ, the Son of the Living God."

In spite of Peter's prominent role, he failed on more than one occasion. The most famous instance occurred during the Lord's trial when, capitulating to the very human emotion of fear, he denied three times even knowing Jesus.

Yet within this impulsive, imperfect, sometimes wavering man, ran a solid gold core of devotion. Despite his failures, it is inspiring the way he kept following the Savior.

John's Gospel tells us that when the risen Lord appeared by the Sea of Tiberius, Peter, repentant, and as optimistic and irrepressible as ever, dived with his coat on from the fishing boat and swam to Him.

There is a marked difference here between Peter and Judas Iscariot. He understood something Judas never comprehended—that a penitent man coming to the Savior can be forgiven. On the shore, Peter's subsequent three-fold, heartfelt expressions of renewed commitment to Jesus erased his denials forever.

Following the Ascension and Pentecost, Peter moved into the leadership of the early church with God-given power, winning 3,000 people to Christ with his first sermon. Tradition and ancient writings indicate that he became one of the foremost missionary evangelists among the disciples.

Toward the end of his ministry, while preaching in Rome, a young man named Mark repeatedly stood beside him, translating his words for the predominantly Greek-speaking Christians. Peter's firsthand memories of Jesus would later provide the substance of Mark's Gospel.

Peter's labors in Rome continually put his life on the line. In approximately A.D. 64, he was martyred—crucified under the persecution of Nero. The massive St. Peter's Church stands on the traditional site of his burial.

Paul may well have had Peter in mind when he wrote his memorable lines, "...if any man be in Christ, he is a new creature."

The Big Fisherman had exploded into discipleship in a chaos of conflicting impulses, fears, and enthusiasms. But the Lord's touch gradually brought order, harmony, and a magnificent stability to his life.

Fulfilling Jesus' vision of strength for him, Peter became as steady as a rock, an immovable man of faith, an inspiration to millions.

JOHN, THE SON OF ZEBEDEE

The word most people associate with John is "love." He was the disciple who, above all others, taught and wrote about Christian love. In his first epistle, the word "love" appears nearly fifty times. But it was not always so with John. He was a man transformed by his association with Jesus.

John emerges from the Gospel pages as an intense and vital man. "Sons of Thunder," the Lord named him and his brother. One can hear a touch of warm, fond humor behind the title. Countering his tendencies toward intolerance, fiery condemnations of others, and self-serving ambition, the Lord won John to a new outlook.

The son of Zebedee, John was James' younger brother. He was probably about eighteen when the two left their fishermen's nets to follow the Lord. With Peter and his brother James, he became one of Jesus' "inner circle."

John identifies himself in his Gospel as, "the disciple whom Jesus loved." In writing this I have a feeling he was expressing amazement and gratitude, not pride. Many Christians today share his wonder as they also discover, "Jesus loves me!"

As John walked with the Lord through Galilee, he became increasingly close to Him. Then in Jerusalem he sat nearest Jesus at the Last Supper. And he alone of the disciples kept vigil at the foot of the cross, where the Savior entrusted to him the care of Mary, His mother.

Following Pentecost, John participated with Peter in the healing of the lame man at the Beautiful Gate of the temple (Acts 3). And it is recorded that they were together on other important occasions, including a trip to Samaria where they ministered to early converts.

Paul describes John as one of the "pillars" of the Jerusalem church. Later, it is believed he took the gospel to Asia Minor, was exiled to the Island of Patmos, and finished his life in Ephesus.

It was during his years in exile and in Ephesus that many believe he wrote the Gospel of John, his three Epistles, and the book of Revelation. The question over whether he actually wrote all, or only part, of these works remains unresolved.

An ancient legend reveals John in old age with the fullness of his natural fire in beautiful harmony with his commitment to Christ. Hearing of a lapsed Christian becoming the leader of a band of thieves, John went after him. Unarmed, the aged Son of Thunder found and entered the criminals' wilderness hiding place and won the recreant back to the Lord.

Tradition says that he lived well into his eighties or nineties, growing so weak at the end he had to be carried into Christian gatherings. Hardly able to speak, John whispered again and again the message that came to be his hallmark, "Little children, love one another."

ANDREW

"Of all the disciples," a friend said to me recently, "Andrew is my favorite." Many would agree.

Although Andrew was one of the quietest, most diffident, and least noticed of The Twelve, he later became the patron saint of three nations—Scotland, Russia, and

Greece. Churches, cities, universities, and a diversity of organizations have been named after him. The influence of this gentle disciple is seen today in the ministry of countless twentieth-century Christians.

Andrew, son of Jona, was Peter's brother. He worked with his family out of Capernaum in a fishing partnership with Zebedee and his sons.

His first move, after meeting Jesus, was to bring his brother Peter to the Lord—an inspiring example to us all. His outreach was greatly rewarded as Peter became a powerful leader among the disciples.

Andrew had a way of inconspicuous service, of background offerings that, given to the Lord, achieved great results. Such was the occasion of the Feeding of the 5,000. Scanning the large crowd, which had followed Him, Jesus asked the disciples how they were going to feed all those people. Philip immediately responded that it would be impossible.

Andrew, however, gravely handed the Lord a small boy's donation of five loaves and three fishes. The disciple's question, "...but what are these among so many?" implies possibility. It reflects an ingenuous openness. Perhaps, somehow, the Lord could use them.

Our hearts are touched by this self-effacing fisherman. As Jesus took, blessed, and fed the multitude through Andrew and the boy's offering, we sense how our gifts can also be used by Him.

One of Andrew's most endearing qualities is found in his reaction to the prominence of Peter. There is no indication that Andrew resented his brother's leadership. He succumbed to no comparisons over who was greatest or most favored. On the contrary, the Gospels reveal a man content to take the supportive role.

It was enough for this unpretentious disciple simply to love, follow, and serve the Lord. He showed an extraordinary grace where his famous brother was concerned, a generosity of soul that is deeply beautiful.

A.A. Milne, the well-known author of the Winnie the Pooh books, had a brother like Andrew. From childhood Milne was by far the more successful of the two. Yet Milne claims his brother was the best of them because of his unfailingly gracious spirit that truly and gladly rejoiced over Milne's triumphs.

According to tradition, Andrew, after Pentecost, carried

the gospel to the wild steppelands of Scythia, north of the Black Sea. It is believed he preached also in Greece where he was martyred for his faith.

Andrew was never known as a great leader. But not all greatness is found in leadership. Vital to the church are the silent, unheralded, faithful thousands who, warm and outreaching like Andrew, quietly bring others to the Lord.

THOMAS

The personality of the Apostle Thomas comes across the centuries with tremendous appeal for us. A realist and a bit of a pessimist, he was committed to honesty. Unafraid to be himself, he frequently displayed resolute courage in the face of known danger.

At the time of Lazarus' death, Thomas and the disciples were appalled by Jesus' determination to go to Bethany. Its proximity to the hostile Pharisees in Jerusalem put Him in grave danger. But Thomas' attitude at this time reflects both his profession, as a carpenter who counts the cost, and his unflinching commitment to Christ.

"Let us also go," he said to the disciples, "that we may die with Him."

Intensely loyal, Thomas was also humble and candid. At the Last Supper, Jesus was trying to help the disciples understand about the resurrection. Thomas listened, his practical mind struggling.

"I go to prepare a place for you," Jesus told them, "And whither I go, ye know and the way ye know."

Suddenly Thomas burst out, "Lord, we know not whither thou goest, and how can we know the way?"

His rock-honest question catalyzed Jesus' answer, "I am the way, the truth and the life." And it is these words that have since illumined the lives of countless millions.

The best known story about Thomas gives him what is perhaps an over-emphasized reputation as a "doubter." When the risen Lord first appeared to the disciples, Thomas was not present. Skeptical, unable to accept their witness, he didn't believe them.

Yet his reservations were part of his earnest quest for truth. Jesus honored his sincerity, appearing again when Thomas was present. Overwhelmed, he whispered, "My Lord and my God."

"Blessed," Jesus responded, "are they that have not seen, and yet have believed."

Gert Behanna, a contemporary Christian who has gone

to be with the Lord, said of her two sons that one crossed the brook to faith effortlessly at the narrow part, while the other labored across where it was widest. Those who come to faith with difficulty find reassuring companionship in Thomas.

After Pentecost, Thomas carried the gospel to foreign lands. Tradition indicates he was martyred and buried in Mylapore, India where a cathedral in his name marks the site.

A legend persists concerning his ministry in India. It appears that King Gundaphorus, hearing of his craftsmanship, contracted with him to construct a palatial residence.

However, during the time Thomas was supposed to be working on the building, he visited surrounding villages instead. He spent all of his time teaching about the love of Christ, healing the sick, and distributing the King's construction funds to the destitute.

When the ruler discovered the apparent fraud, Thomas was imprisoned, pending execution. The King's brother, falling ill at this time, had a vision of a beautiful palace built in heaven for Gundaphorus by Thomas' good works. Hearing of the dream, the King summoned Thomas, heard his testimony, and was converted.

Whatever the legend's accuracy, it well represents the spirit of Thomas, a carpenter builder for the Kingdom of Heaven.

MATTHEW

Matthew's story is especially moving. Believed to be also known as Levi, the son of Alphaeus, he was a tax collector.

The publicans or tax gatherers were hated by the Jews because of their collaboration with the Romans. Their word was not accepted in Jewish courts, and their offerings were refused in the synagogue. In fact, they were even excluded from participation in worship services. A pious Pharisee would not marry into the family of a publican.

The collectors were infamous not only for exacting taxes for the Romans, but for the fat profits they realized for themselves in the process. "Brothers to Vultures," they were called.

Matthew was most likely literate, orderly, trained in keeping records, and comfortably prosperous. Yet, deep in his heart, there must have been a hunger for something better. Perhaps he had stood in the crowds on the shore and heard Jesus speak. Possibly he had witnessed some of the healings in Capernaum. Whatever it was, his captivity to unscrupulous money-making evidently began to crumble, for when the Lord came to him in the customs office, Matthew left everything to follow Him.

His first move as a disciple was to give a dinner party. He invited the only people who would have anything to do with him—tax collectors and their associates—with Jesus as his honored guest.

The scribes and Pharisees criticized the Savior for attending. The Lord, however, joined the outcasts' dinner, not to affirm them as they were, but to offer wholeness. His response to His critics provides insight into the way He looked at Matthew and his colleagues.

"They that are whole," He said, "need not a physician; but they that are sick." He regarded the publicans' bondage to avarice as a doctor regards illness—not something to be condemned, but cured.

The Lord's beautiful parables about the Treasure in the Field and The Pearl must have impressed Matthew deeply, for his is the only Gospel that records them. As Matthew left behind his lucrative but dishonorable trade, he knew firsthand what it meant to abandon "all that he had" for the Pearl of Great Price.

Although Scripture tells us little more about Matthew, tradition places him ministering to the Hebrews in Judea after Pentecost. Accounts of his death conflict. It is possible that he passed away peacefully in old age.

Matthew's great legacy to us is the Gospel that bears his name. And while it isn't generally believed that he was the sole author, most scholars agree that he was responsible for a significant part of this careful record of the sayings and teachings of Jesus.

There are those who believe that just as Jesus gave Simon the name of Peter, so He gave Levi the name Matthew, meaning "Gift of God." Truly, the once despised tax collector was transformed by the hand of the Lord into becoming a Gift from God.

JUDAS ISCARIOT

On the Gospel lists of the disciples, Judas Iscariot is cited by Matthew and Mark as Jesus' betrayer and by Luke as the "traitor." His background, his motive for the betrayal, and even the circumstances of his death remain somewhat mysterious.

His name may provide some enlightenment about him.

One interpretation of "Iscariot" is "man from Kerioth." If Judas came from this Judaean village, he would have been the only non-Galilean disciple. It may have been that he continually felt like an outsider. But considering the warmth of the disciples and their commitment to good-will, it could be that any sense of estrangement Judas might have felt came from his own bitter imagination.

A painting by Andrea del Costagno in Florence, Italy, portrays Judas and the disciples at the Last Supper. His isolation from the group is sharply defined. The artist painted him as the only one without a glow of light about his head; instead, the forces of darkness appear to war in his countenance. He sits alone, across the table from the others.

It is believed by many that the reason Judas betrayed Jesus was tied to his original purpose in following Him. In the tremendous power and magnetism of the Lord, Judas may have believed he had found the Messiah who would overthrow Roman rule and establish a mighty Jewish Kingdom.

During the Lord's ministry, he was perhaps increasingly baffled, frustrated, and angered until finally, he became totally disillusioned with Jesus. He then turned traitor because of his resentment and disappointment.

Although this is a possibility, Judas' motives remain obscure. Some believe he meant well all along, that through the betrayal he was trying to force the Lord to take action, summon supporters, and become a national hero and king.

Others claim that Judas' motives were those of a common scoundrel, that he was a thief, as John's Gospel reports, that he simply wanted the money.

Whatever his reasons, Judas Iscariot betrayed his Lord for thirty pieces of silver. It was through Judas' duplicity that Jesus was identified and arrested in the garden by the soldiers that had been sent by the chief priests and Pharisees.

One can't help but feel an ache for Judas as he became aware of the enormity of what he had done. It is heartrending to read of his remorse as he tried to return the money to the chief priests and elders, throwing the coins on the temple floor when they refused it.

His death, either by hanging himself as reported by Matthew, or by falling "headlong" as reported in Acts, projects an image of inconsolable despair.

As we look back to this tragic story of Judas, we shrink in horror from any identification with him or his infamous deed. And yet we are forced to say, "There, but for the grace of God, am I."

PHILIP

In his Gospel, John makes it clear that Philip of Bethsaida was someone the Lord especially selected for discipleship. "Jesus," John wrote, "...findeth Philip, and saith unto him, 'Follow me.'"

Since Philip came from Bethsaida, it is possible he was a fisherman. It is believed that he was married and had several daughters and that he possibly had been a follower of John the Baptist.

An eleventh-century mosaic depicts him as beardless, young looking, with large, dark, observant eyes and an uncertain air. Scripture reveals him as having been pragmatic, balanced, commonsensical, and cautious.

Philip's first act as a disciple was to tell his friend, Nathanael, that he had found the Messiah. Since Nathanael reacted with skepticism, Philip sensibly suggested he "Come and see."

Philip's down-to-earth handling of a skeptic is as realistic today as it was then. Several years ago, a university student expressed to a minister his doubts about the Christian faith. "Don't worry about your uncertainties," the clergyman advised, "Just follow the Lord. He will reveal Himself to you." The young man, like Nathanael, ultimately became a person of deep faith.

Philip expressed his practical nature at the time of the Feeding of the Five Thousand. When Jesus saw the crowd gathered around Him in the hills, he specifically asked Philip where they could buy bread to feed the multitude.

The disciple responded in character. Taking into account the amount of bread needed, he decided it was impossible for them to feed the crowd.

So many times our own estimates tell us the same. Like Philip, we haven't enough. Maybe we're short of strength or we haven't the love a situation requires. Perhaps our time is too short or our resources inadequate. Then we remember Jesus meeting the need despite the obvious insufficiency. The story provides a guiding star.

Philip wasn't bold, but hesitant. When certain Greeks came to him wanting to meet Jesus, he first took them to

Andrew. The two of them then introduced the foreigners to the Lord.

The Greeks' opening words to Philip remain thought-provoking to this day. "Sir," they said, "We would see Jesus." In a church in Texas, their request is inscribed on the pulpit where whoever preaches cannot miss it.

Philip was not spiritually perceptive. His matter-of-fact mind labored over the Lord's teachings. At the Last Supper, unable to follow Jesus' words, he interrupted with, "Lord, show us the Father and it sufficeth us." Jesus gave His infinitely wise answer, "...he that hath seen me hath seen the Father."

It is no wonder, though, that the Savior selected Philip to be His disciple. It is through His guidance of this pragmatic disciple that He guides us all.

There are many legends associated with Philip in his years after Pentecost, but we know virtually nothing for sure about him. It is important that we not associate him with another Philip mentioned in the Book of Acts who was a deacon and evangelist.

SIMON THE ZEALOT

The image revealed in Scripture of Simon the Zealot is of an enthusiast who may have had a most unusual background for a disciple.

Simon was designated "the Zealot" either because of his earnest, fervent nature or, for the more likely reason, that he had been associated with the Zealots.

The Zealots, fanatical Jewish patriots, were bitterly opposed to Roman rule in Palestine. Driven by hatred and a passion for Jewish law, they burned and plundered homes and villages using hit-and-run tactics, killing and terrorizing not only Romans but any of their own countrymen suspected of collaboration. In many ways they were akin to modern terrorists. Their code and lifestyle provided unlikely nurture for a future disciple of the loving Savior.

Simon has been described as striding into Christian discipleship with a sword in his hand, his clothes still smoking from the latest Zealot raid.

If it is true that he was, in fact, a member of the rebel patriots, then he underwent a powerful conversion experience through his contact with the Lord. A fresh breeze of God's love would have cleared the bitterness from his soul. Revenge would have given way to forgiveness, and brutality to mercy. Simon's sense of relief as he was released from the tyranny of hatred, and moved into warm, affectionate, peaceful relationships must have been profound.

It is incredible to picture this former Zealot sitting down to eat and pray with Matthew, the former tax collector and collaborator with the Romans. Surely, this is evidence of one of those miracles Jesus can bring about in the area of otherwise impossible relationships.

The depth of Simon's conversion may have been sorely tested when the Lord sent His disciples out by two's to preach and heal. It appears that Simon was paired with Judas Iscariot. The two would have spent long hours together. As they walked and talked along the dusty roads, perhaps Simon lapsed into a disturbed and thoughtful silence as he suspected that Judas' heart was frozen against the message of the Lord.

Faithful through the Lord's ministry, Simon received the Holy Spirit at Pentecost. Tradition tells us he spread the gospel in Armenia with Thaddaeus. Some accounts claim he was martyred there, others that he died peacefully in Edessa.

It is possible that Simon was the disciple most changed by Christ. One wishes there were more information about him. Nevertheless, Scripture and legend paint a picture of a man zealous, not for revenge nor the exercise of hate, but for the love of God.

JAMES, THE SON OF ZEBEDEE

A painting by Edward Armitage portrays James, his brother, and father, motionless in their fishing boat, with their gaze fixed on the Lord who beckons from the shore. The commanding power the artist conveys through Jesus' form is spellbinding. And it is history that the two brothers, in the words of Luke's Gospel, "...forsook all, and followed Him."

Vitality and courage wave like a banner over the story of James. He took quite a risk when he left the successful family business in Capernaum to follow Jesus. The expression "stepping out on faith" well applies to him.

One of the two named "Sons of Thunder" by Jesus, James shared his brother John's high-spirited, hotheaded temperament. Fishing was a rough trade, with treacherous storms to face on the sea and stiff competitors on land. James must have been weathered and fit, and inwardly tough when he met the Lord.

On one occasion, swept by a wave of anger, he urged Jesus to call down fire from heaven to consume the inhabitants of an unfriendly Samaritan village.

At another time, self-seeking ambition drove him to join John in requesting that the two be given the favored places in the Lord's coming kingdom.

In both instances, Jesus overturned James' outlook, leading him into fresh, new ways of thinking. The Lord and His followers were to save, not destroy; to serve, not dominate.

As one of Jesus' most favored disciples, James was a witness with Peter and John of both the Transfiguration and the restoring to life of Jairus' daughter.

He was one of the three the Savior took with Him to pray in the Garden of Gethsemane. A painting of this scene by Mantegna shows Jesus, on the left of the picture, praying in anguish of soul. In the center James, along with Peter and John, are sprawled asleep on the ground, and to the right is a wooden bridge. A wild rabbit poised on the bridge listens with ears cocked. In the distance comes "the great multitude armed with swords and staves" led by Judas Iscariot. In this poignant painting James' humanity is so clearly represented as all unknowing, he sleeps.

Following Pentecost, James became one of the foremost leaders of the Jerusalem church. Legend indicates he also made missionary journeys to Spain. However, his courageous and powerful ministry was short-lived as he was the first disciple to be martyred. He was executed by Herod Agrippa, King of Palestine, in A.D. 42.

Ancient historians have left us a moving account of his last minutes. It seems that his chief accuser, deeply affected by James' conduct and testimony during his trial, was converted.

As James was led to his execution, the new believer begged his forgiveness. Following a moment of silence, the Son of Thunder turned and gently said, "Peace be with thee."

NATHANAEL BARTHOLOMEW

On first sight, Bartholomew appears to be only a faceless name on a series of New Testament lists of the disciples. However, there are sound reasons to believe that the

Bartholomew listed in the first three Gospels and Acts is also the interesting Nathanael of the fourth Gospel.

Since the ninth century, it has been widely accepted that this disciple was named in full, Nathanael Bar-Tolmai (Son of Tolmai), just as Peter was named Simon Bar-Jona (Son of Jona). The name Bartholomew means Son of Tolmai.

Nathanael Bartholomew first became aware of the Lord in his home village of Cana in Galilee. His friend, Philip, burst upon him with the news that a certain "Jesus of Nazareth" was the Messiah.

Nathanael's reaction was skeptical. "Can any good thing come out of Nazareth?" he asked.

One gets an impression of disdain, of someone who considered himself to be a bit superior, of a touch of pride and a raised eyebrow. Nathanael had not yet been influenced by the humbling love of Christ. But following Philip's suggestion, Nathanael went to see this Jesus for himself. The experience shattered his doubts forever.

The Lord met him with the words, "Behold an Israelite in whom there is no guile!" His perception must have been most accurate, for Nathanael immediately asked how Jesus could know him so well.

The Lord's answer, that He had seen him under the spreading shade of the fig tree, ignited Nathanael's faith in sudden flame. Thunderstruck, he responded, "Rabbi, thou art the Son of God." Jesus must have identified some intensely personal and private experience, probably in prayer, which Nathanael was convinced only God could have known about.

This disciple, whose heart held no secrets from Jesus, followed Him faithfully through His earthly ministry. Several times he witnessed the risen Lord and, after Pentecost, he courageously carried the faith into foreign lands. Armenia considers him one of the principle founders of the church there. His name is also linked with India.

Christian visitors to India, as early as A.D. 150, found that native converts already possessed a copy of Matthew's Gospel, which they said had been given them by Nathanael Bartholomew. There are traditions both in India and Armenia concerning his martyrdom.

Nathanael, from the little village of Cana, was the first, but not the last, to move from reserved skepticism concerning the divinity of Jesus, to profound life-changing certainty.

JAMES, THE SON OF ALPHAEUS

James, the son of Alphaeus, must have been quiet and reserved. Appearing only in the New Testament as a name on the lists of the disciples, his personality at first seems hidden. However, like gold, he is well worth searching out and, once found, he shines.

He followed the Lord throughout His ministry, crucifixion, and resurrection. And in the Book of Acts, he is listed among those present in the Upper Room at Pentecost who received the Holy Spirit.

There is speculation that he was Matthew's brother. Matthew, also called Levi, had a father named Alphaeus. And it is possible that his mother was a follower of Jesus. Mark writes in his Gospel of a "Mary the mother of James the Less..." who witnessed the crucifixion.

"James the Less" may have been an affectionate title describing James' youth or lack of stature. It is also possible the title was used to differentiate him from James, the son of Zebedee or James, the "brother" of the Lord, both of whom became outstanding figures in the early church.

Legend reveals little more about this disciple than Scripture does. There is a faint tradition that he was martyred while spreading the gospel in Persia.

Yet through this very lack of information, James' character emerges. For instance, there is no record that he ever made demands, caused an uproar, or was rebuked by the Lord for his blundering as was the case with many of the other disciples.

One gets the impression of a careful, thoughtful person, someone who stayed in the background and kept things going. He was probably much loved and depended on by the more prominent disciples.

James would have understood that Jesus calls His followers not to eminence but to service. He must have experienced that freeing peace and joy of heart the Savior imparts to those who follow Him in humility and simplicity. The ongoing strength of Christianity is found in people such as James.

When we look at our churches, we find members who remind us of this disciple. Unpretentious, constant, silent as light—they glow in our midst.

My husband's mother was one of them. She never sought center stage or showed any desire for prominence.

She simply gave her best to the job at hand, whatever it might be. Steadfast amidst the turmoil of this world, she stood and lived like a rock for the Lord. Her family and friends drew unceasing strength and inspiration from her. Yet, she was barely known outside her small hometown.

James, the son of Alphaeus must have been similar, one of the Lord's most blessed Quiet Faithful ones.

THADDAEUS

Thaddaeus was also known as Lebbaeus and as Judas, the son of James. Thaddaeus was his surname and Lebbaeus may have been a descriptive name meaning "large-hearted." The King James Version of the Bible calls him the "brother" of James, but in later translations this has been changed to "son."

Although the first three Gospels give only his name, he appears in the fourth Gospel questioning the Lord. His words have the ring of sincerity, of a man earnestly seeking to understand. Jesus treats him as such and responds with a deep and thought-provoking answer.

The scene of the exchange was the Last Supper. Judas Iscariot was no longer present. The Lord, having told the remaining eleven disciples that He would be going away and the world would see Him no more, promised that, nevertheless, *they* would see Him. And He added that He would show Himself to those who kept His commandments.

Thaddaeus, puzzled, asked, "Lord, how is it...thou wilt manifest thyself unto us, and not unto the world?"

The Savior repeated what He had said before, this time using expressions that were easier to understand, more homespun. "If a man loves me," He answered, "he will keep my words: and my Father will love him, and we will come unto him and make our abode with him."

The promise was swiftly realized. Following the crucifixion, it was to the disciples, men who had made deep commitments to Him, that the risen Lord revealed Himself. And to this day, the mystical sense of His Presence strengthens those who love and follow Him.

Beyond his question at the Last Supper, Scripture tells little more about Thaddaeus. According to tradition, he carried the gospel to Armenia and Persia, working and traveling with Simon the Zealot. It is believed he was martyred in Armenia and buried in Edessa.

An ancient legend remains concerning him, recorded as factual by Eusebius, fourth-century Bishop of Caesarea. It seems that during the Lord's earthly ministry King Abgar of Mesopotamia contracted a serious illness. Hearing of the healing miracles of Jesus, he believed Him to be the Son of God.

King Abgar sent a letter from his residence in Edessa to Jesus by a courier named Ananias, imploring the Lord to come and heal him. Jesus is said to have returned a message to the ruler by Ananias, commending Abgar for his faith and promising that one of the disciples would come to him.

Following the Ascension, Thaddaeus went to the king. Through the power of the risen Lord, he healed him and won a substantial number of converts. Refusing money pressed on him by the grateful ruler, he left Edessa to carry his ministry further.

The little information available concerning Thaddaeus suggests that he was a sincere, earnest, true-blue kind of man. One wishes he had left his autobiography. But the disciples were interested in only one biography, as they carried the story of Jesus to the world. The life and work of Thaddaeus point not to himself, but to the Lord.

A personal note from the author

Years ago, I attended a retreat in which the participants were asked to each find a quiet place and there, in solitude, prayerfully recall the people God had used to bring them to Him.

Among the many who came to mind, I especially remembered a certain Sunday School teacher. There had been a glow of loving kindness about her which had deeply drawn me to the Lord about whom she spoke.

Such were the disciples of Jesus. In them He shined as a candle in the night and from them the Light of His glory passed on to touch hearts, one after another, down through the ages, for all eternity.

SPECIFIC MIRACLES IN THE GOSPEL OF MARK

1. Jesus heals a demon-possessed man in the Synagogue at Capernaum — 1:23–27
2. Jesus heals the fever of Peter's mother-in-law — 1:29–31
3. Jesus heals a leper — 1:40–45
4. A paralyzed man healed at Capernaum — 2:3–12
5. Jesus heals the man with a withered hand — 3:1–6
6. Jesus calms the storm on the Sea of Galilee — 4:35–41
7. Jesus heals the demon-possessed man of Gadara — 5:2–20
8. Jesus restores life to Jairus' daughter in Capernaum — 5:22; 35–43
9. Jesus heals a woman with a hemorrhage in Capernaum — 5:25–34
10. The feeding of the 5,000 with five loaves and two fish — 6:35–44
11. Jesus walks on the water (Sea of Galilee) — 6:45–52
12. Jesus heals the daughter of a Canaanite (Syrophoenician) woman in the region of Tyre and Sidon — 7:24–30
13. Jesus heals a deaf man with a speech impediment — 7:32–37
14. The feeding of the 4,000 with seven loaves and a few fish — 8:1–10
15. Jesus heals a blind man at Bethsaida — 8:22–26
16. Jesus heals a lunatic (demon-possessed) boy — 9:17–29
17. Jesus restores sight to a blind beggar (Bartimaeus) on the Jericho road — 10:46–52
18. At Jesus' command the barren fig tree dies — 11:12–14; 20–22

THE PARABLES OF JESUS IN MARK

1. The Parable of the Sower and the Soils — 4:3–20
2. The Parable of the Seed That Grows — 4:26–29
3. The Parable of the Mustard Seed — 4:30–32
4. The Parable of the Rented Vineyard — 12:1–12

A HARMONY OF THE GOSPELS

	MATTHEW	MARK	LUKE	JOHN
The genealogy of Jesus	1:1–17		3:23–38	
The birth of John the Baptist			1:5–25, 57–80	
The birth of Jesus	1:5–25; 2:1		2:1–20	
The wise men find Jesus	2:1–12			
The flight to Egypt	2:13–23			
The boy Jesus at the temple			2:41–50	
John the Baptist preaches and baptizes	3:1–12	1:1–8	3:1–20	
Jesus' baptism	3:13–17	1:9–11	3:21–22	
Jesus' temptation	4:1–11	1:12–13	4:1–13	
Jesus' first miracle at Cana				2:1–11
Jesus and Nicodemus				3:1–21
Jesus and the Samaritan woman				4:5–42
Jesus heals the nobleman's son				4:46–54
Jesus selects four disciples	4:18–22	1:16–20	5:1–11	
Demon-possessed man healed		1:23–28	4:31–37	
Jesus gives the Sermon on the Mount	5:1–7:29		6:20–49	
The parable of the two builders	7:24–27		6:47–49	
Jesus heals a leper	8:1–4	1:40–45	5:12–14	
The centurion's servant healed	8:5–13		7:1–10	
Peter's mother-in-law healed	8:14–15	1:29–31	4:38–39	
Life restored to the widow's son			7:11–17	
Jesus calms the storm	8:23–27	4:36–41	8:22–25	
Demon-possessed men healed	8:28–34	5:1–21	8:26–40	
Paralyzed man healed	9:1–8	2:3–12	5:18–26	
Life restored to Jairus' daughter	9:18–19, 23–26	5:22–24, 35–43	8:41–42, 49–56	
Woman healed of hemorrhage	9:20–22	5:25–34	8:43–48	
Blind man healed (Capernaum)	9:27–31			
Devil cast out of dumb man	9:32–34			

Event	Matthew	Mark	Luke	John
The disciples sent on tour	10:1—11:1	6:7-13	9:1-6	
Man with withered hand healed	12:9-14	3:1-5	6:6-11	
The parable of the sower	13:4-9, 18-23	4:1-20	8:14-15	
The parable of the tares	13:24-30			
The parable of the mustard seed	13:31-32	4:30-32		
The parable of the leaven	13:33-34		13:20-21	
The parable of hidden treasure	13:44			
The parable of the pearl	13:45			
The parable of the net	13:47-50			
John the Baptist killed	14:1-12	6:14-29	9:7-9	
The feeding of the 5,000	14:13-21	6:33-44	9:11-17	6:1-14
Jesus walks on the sea	14:22-33	6:45-52		6:15-21
Canaanite woman's daughter healed	15:21-28	7:24-30		
The feeding of the 4,000	15:32-38	8:1-9		
Blind man at Bethsaida healed		8:22-26		
Peter's great confession	16:13-26	8:27-37	9:18-25	
The transfiguration of Jesus	16:27—17:13	8:38—9:13	9:26-36	
Lunatic boy healed	17:14-21	9:14-29	9:37-43	
Tax money from fish's mouth	17:24-27			
The parable of the wealthy farmer			12:16-21	
Crippled woman healed			13:10-13	
The parable of the lost sheep	18:12-13		15:3-7	
The parable of the lost coin			15:8-10	
The parable of the prodigal son			15:11-32	
The parable of the unmerciful servant	18:23-35			
Jesus and the rich young ruler	19:16—20:16	10:17-31	18:18-30	
The adulterous woman				8:1-11
Man born blind healed				9:1-41
The parable of the good shepherd				10:1-18
The parable of the good Samaritan			10:30-37	
The parable of the friend at midnight			11:5-10	

Chart Continued on Following Page

	MATTHEW	MARK	LUKE	JOHN
The parable of the good father			11:11–13	
Lazarus raised from the dead				11:1–44
Jesus heals ten lepers			17:11–19	
The parable of the laborers in the vineyard	20:1–16			
Jesus heals the blind men	20:29–34	10:46–52	18:35–43	
Jesus and the barren fig tree	21:18–22	11:12–14, 20–26		
The parable of the man with two sons	21:28–32			
Jesus and Zacchaeus			19:1–10	
The parable of the landowner	21:33–44	12:1–9	20:9–19	
The triumphal entry of Jesus	21:1–11	11:1–10	19:29–40	12:12–19
Jesus clears the temple	21:12–13	11:15–19	19:45–48	
The parable of the marriage feast	22:1–14		14:16–24	
The parable of the fig tree	24:32	13:28–31	21:29–33	
The parable of the virgins	25:1–13			
The parable of the man, his servants, and the talents	25:14–30			
Jesus looks ahead to His crucifixion	26:1–5	14:1–2	22:1–2	
Mary anoints Jesus	26:6–13	14:3–9		12:2–8
Judas plots with authorities	26:14–16	14:10–11	22:3–6	
Last Passover and the Lord's Supper	26:20–29	14:17–21	22:7–30	
Jesus in Gethsemane	26:36–46	14:32–42	22:39–46	18:1
Betrayal and arrest of Jesus	26:47–56	14:43–52	22:47–53	18:2–12
Jesus' trial before Caiaphas and the Sanhedrin	26:57–68	14:55–65	22:63–65	18:24
Peter denies Jesus	26:69–75	14:66–72	22:54–62	18:15–18
Jesus' trial before Pilate	27:11–26	15:1–15	23:1–25	18:28–40; 19:1–15
The crucifixion of Jesus	27:33–56	15:22–41	23:33–49	19:16–30
The burial of Jesus	27:57–61	15:42–47	23:50–56	19:38–42
The resurrection of Jesus	28:1–10	16:1–7	24:1–12	20:1–10
Post-resurrection appearances	28:9–10, 16–20	16:9–18	24:13–48	20:11–29; 21:1–22
The ascension of Jesus		16:19–20	24:50–53	

THE PALESTINE OF JESUS' TIME

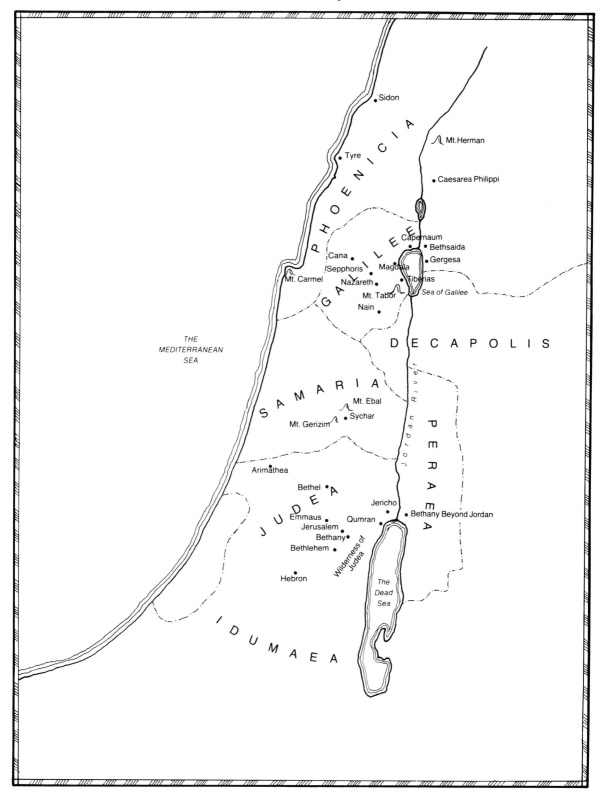

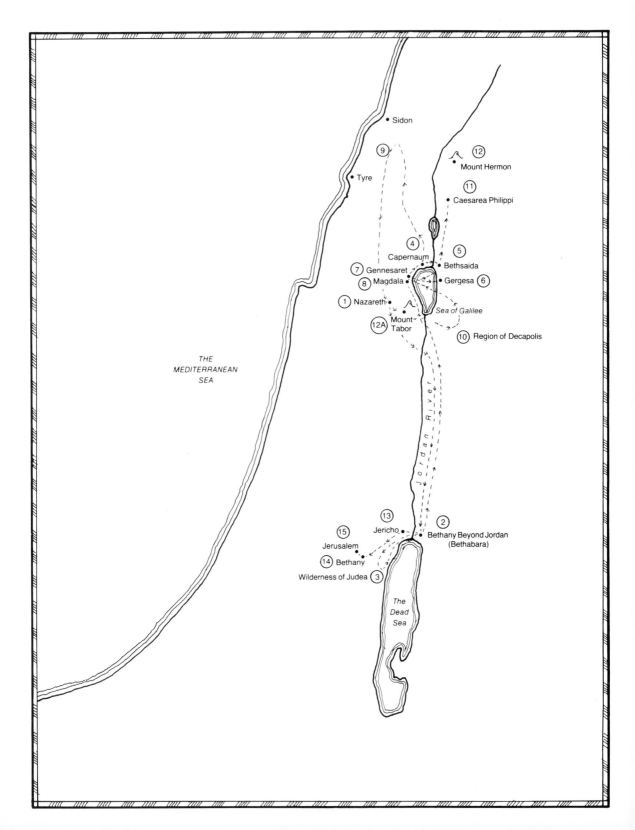

THE TRAVELS OF JESUS IN THE GOSPEL OF MARK

The Gospel of Mark begins the story of Jesus' travels as He leaves Nazareth ① (Mark 1:9) and heads south, probably along the Jordan Valley route, east of the Jordan River, to Bethany Beyond Jordan (Bethabara) ② where He is baptized by John the Baptist (Mark 1:10–11). From there He moves into the Wilderness of Judea ③ and endures temptation by the devil for a period of forty days (Mark 1:12–13).

It is quite likely that on His return north He retraces His steps along the Jordan River and moves around the Sea of Galilee to the north shore to Capernaum ④ and Bethsaida ⑤ where He calls Simon and Andrew and James and John to be His disciples (Mark 1:16–20). Then in the synagogue at Capernaum ④ He heals the demon-possessed man, and in the home of Simon Peter He heals Peter's mother-in-law of a fever (Mark 1:21–31). From there He travels throughout the cities and villages of Galilee preaching and healing (Mark 1:38–45).

Jesus then returned to Capernaum ④ where He continued His preaching and healing ministry (Mark 2—4:34). He then crossed the Sea of Galilee to the country of the Gerasenes, probably Gergesa ⑥ where He healed the demoniac (Mark 4:35—5:1–20). Upon returning to Capernaum ④ He restored Jairus' daughter to life and healed the woman with a hemorrhage (Mark 5:21–43).

After a visit to Nazareth ① (Mark 6:1–6), Jesus toured several villages and returned to Capernaum ④. Following the feeding of the 5,000, probably near Bethsaida ⑤ (Mark 6:30–44) He crossed the Sea of Galilee to Gennesaret ⑦ (Mark 6:53–55), most likely located on the western shore a short distance north of Magdala ⑧. From there He probably worked His way back around the Sea of Galilee to Capernaum ④ (Mark 6:56—7:23).

Next, Jesus traveled north and west to the region of Tyre and Sidon ⑨ where He healed the daughter of the Syrophoenician—Canaanite—woman (Mark 7:24–30). On His return He probably moved south through the heart of Galilee around the lower end of the sea into the region of Decapolis ⑩ where He healed the deaf and dumb man and miraculously fed the 4,000 with seven loaves and a few small fish (Mark 7:31—8:10). Immediately after the feeding of the 4,000 Jesus and His disciples crossed the Sea of Galilee to Dalmanutha, thought to be Magdala ⑧. From there, they moved back across the sea to Bethsaida ⑤ (Mark 8:10–26).

Jesus and His disciples then traveled north to Caesarea Philippi ⑪ where Peter made his great profession of faith (Mark 8:27–30). From there Jesus took Peter, James, and John up to the mountain where He was transfigured—two sites for the Mount of Transfiguration are suggested: Mount Hermon ⑫, just to the north of Caesarea Philippi and Mount Tabor ⑫ᴀ located east of Nazareth ① a short distance. They then returned to Capernaum ④ (Mark 9:33).

Next, we see Jesus and His disciples moving south, probably traveling down the Jordan Valley on the east side of the river to the vicinity of Bethabara ② (Mark 10:1). After ministering there for a time, they cross the Jordan to Jericho ⑬ where He heals Bartimaeus (Mark 10:32–52). They then move west up the road to Bethany ⑭ and then into Jerusalem ⑮ (Mark 11:1–11). From there on through the rest of the Gospel, Jesus' activities center around Jerusalem ⑮ and its environs (Mark 11:12—16:20).

JERUSALEM/JERICHO ENVIRONS

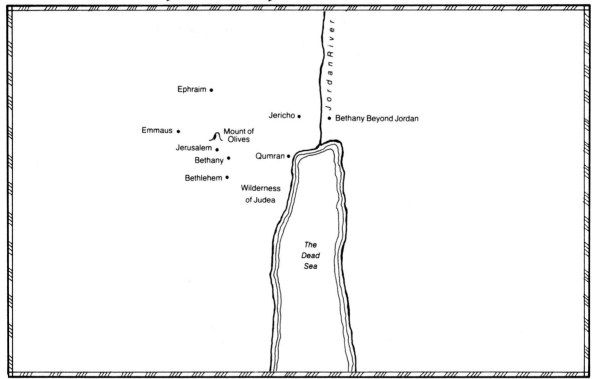

Ephraim •

Jericho •
        • Bethany Beyond Jordan

Jordan River

Emmaus •   ~ Mount of
              Olives
Jerusalem •
    Bethany •   Qumran •

Bethlehem •

Wilderness
of Judea

*The
Dead
Sea*

GALILEE

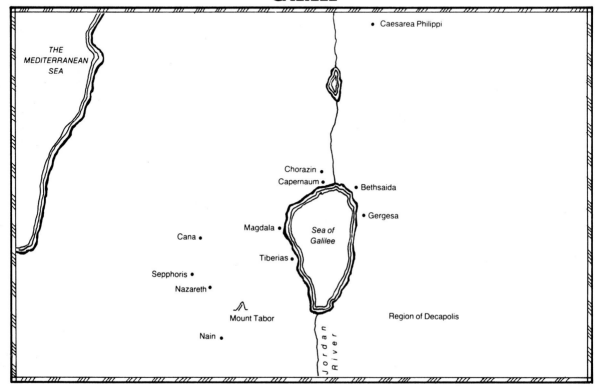

*THE
MEDITERRANEAN
SEA*

    • Caesarea Philippi

Chorazin •
Capernaum •   • Bethsaida

            • Gergesa

Cana •   Magdala •   *Sea of
Galilee*

Sepphoris •   Tiberias •

Nazareth •

    ~ Mount Tabor

              Region of Decapolis

Nain •

*Jordan
River*